ISABELLA TREE was born in 1964. She studied Classics at London University, where she won several prizes for Latin and Greek. She has worked as news editor of the *Geographical Magazine*, and as travel correspondent of the *Evening Standard* has travelled extensively among all seven continents. She now works as a freelance journalist and contributing editor for the *Evening Standard Magazine*, and is a scuba diver and pilot. In 1991 the Society of Authors awarded her a grant to write about Papua New Guinea. Isabella is also the author of *The Ruling Passion of John Gould*, a biography of the Victorian ornithologist.

D1310248

The island of New Guinea lies just north of Australia, in the south-west Pacific. It is divided into independent Papua New Guinea in the east and Irian Jaya in the west. Irian Jaya is a province of Indonesia.

ISLANDS IN THE CLOUDS

Travels in the Highlands of New Guinea

Isabella Tree

LONELY PLANET PUBLICATIONS
Melbourne • Oakland • London • Paris

Islands in the Clouds: Travels in the Highlands of New Guinea

Published by Lonely Planet Publications

    Head Office: PO Box 617, Hawthorn, Vic 3122, Australia
    Branches: 155 Filbert St, Suite 251, Oakland, CA 94607, USA
                 10 Barley Mow Passage, Chiswick, London W4 4PH, UK
                 71 bis rue du Cardinal Lemoine, 75005 Paris, France

Published 1996

Printed by SNP Printing Pte Ltd, Singapore

Author photograph by Charlie Burrell

Maps by Trudi Canavan

National Library of Australia Cataloguing in Publication Data

Tree, Isabella, 1964-
Islands in the Clouds: Travels in the Highlands of New Guinea

ISBN 0 86442 369 1.

1. Tree, Isabella, 1964- – Journeys – Papua New Guinea.
2. Tree, Isabella, 1964- – Journeys – Indonesia – Irian Jaya.
3. Papua New Guinea – Description and travel.
4. Irian Jaya (Indonesia) – Description and travel.
5. Papua New Guinea – Social life and customs.
6. Irian Jaya (Indonesia) – Social life and customs.
I. Title (Series: Lonely Planet Journeys).

995.5

Text © Isabella Tree 1996
Maps © Lonely Planet 1996

For Charlie, who married me in Papua New Guinea

ACKNOWLEDGMENTS

The author and publisher would like to thank the following for permission to quote copyright material:

The *Sydney Morning Herald* for the extract on page 18; the *Independent on Sunday* for the extract on page 52; the *Post Courier* for the extract on pages 65-66; Hank Nelson and the Australian Broadcasting Corporation for the extract from *Taim Bilong Masta* (ABC Books, 1982) on page 116.

CONTENTS

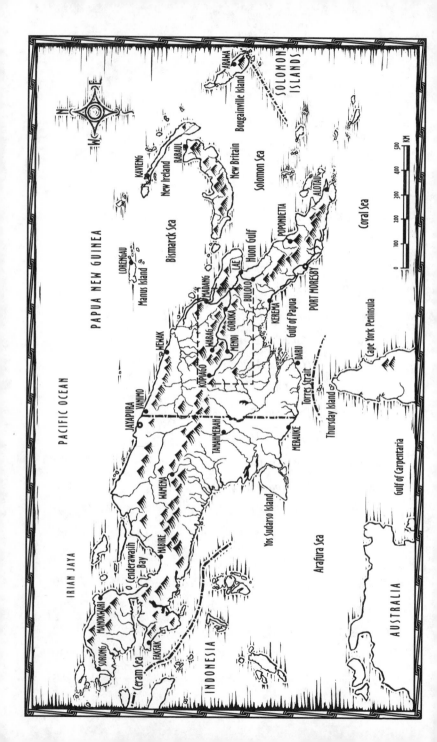

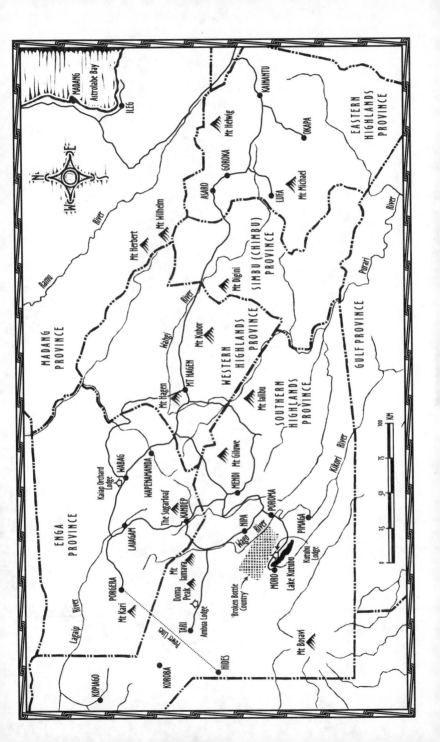

PREFACE

Islands in the Clouds

There was once a rumour circulating the royal courts of Europe about a wild, fantastic land on the other side of the world where birds lit up the sky like rainbows. Though the land was all forest, these birds with shimmering plumes and tail feathers a yard long did not roost in the treetops. They made their nests in the clouds.

Incredible though the story seemed, the sceptical were shown bird skins, remarkably preserved (especially compared with the specimens arriving from South America), their colours as brilliant as the day they had last flown. A few bore the mark of the arrow that had killed them. But many were without blemish, almost as if they had volunteered their bodies for the curiosity of Europe.

But the most surprising thing about the specimens was that none of them had feet or legs – leading to the conclusion that 'birds of paradise', as they became known, lived their entire life on the wing. They sported an unusual complement of feathers – capes, fans and long, draping tails, even a second pair of wings attached to the breast – all the better, it seemed, for keeping their bodies permanently in the heavens.

The first five specimens of the bird of paradise were brought to Europe early in the sixteenth century by one of Ferdinand Magellan's ships returning to Spain after circumnavigating the globe. By the nineteenth century, skins in their thousands were finding their way into museums and private collections. Their feathers danced in the streets of London and Paris on the hats of fashionable ladies, much as they were worn in the head-dresses of the 'cannibals' who had killed them.

But the first eyewitness account of a living bird of paradise was not recorded until 1824, and that was nearly fifty years before any Europeans considered settling in New Guinea.

The island of New Guinea – six times the size of England – is the second largest island in the world after Greenland. It is the product of one of the earth's most violent geological upheavals, the tremors of which shake the place daily, sending gasps of protest from one or more of the dozens of live volcanoes. It lies on the volcanic rim of the great Pacific 'ring of fire', at the point where the northbound Indian-Australian tectonic plate collides with four or five Pacific plates moving south.

The impact has produced the highest mountains in the eastern hemisphere after the Himalayas. Many of them are over 10,000 feet; the highest is 16,500. This is the only island in the tropics which can boast a range of peaks covered permanently in snow.

The mountains are also responsible for the island's excessive rainfall – on average sixty inches a year. In some places, two hundred and eighty inches can fall annually. The result, in the low-lying coastal regions, is uninterrupted rainforest: impenetrable, humid, ridden with mosquitoes, and the only obvious resemblance (apart from the fuzzy-haired people the Portuguese called 'Los Papuas') that New Guinea ever bore to its African namesake.

To the imperial powers in Europe, ever on the look-out for new claims, New Guinea was low on the list. Early explorers reported no signs of mineral wealth or agricultural potential, and trial colonies were wiped out by a myriad unaccountable tropical diseases.

As violent and inhospitable as the geography itself were the indigenous islanders. Settlers were warned off the country by remarks entered on the map by their predecessors: 'natives unfriendly'; 'local population dangerous and unpredictable'; 'site of previous attacks'. There were more rewarding places to invest in, it seemed, than tropical New Guinea.

It was not until 1848, the year of the great revolutions in Europe, that the Dutch, deciding to extend their influence in the East Indies, officially declared sovereignty over the western side of the island. Little knowing the far-reaching consequences of their act, they drew an arbitrary boundary straight through the middle of the island down the 141st meridian.

Even then, other colonial powers, usually quick as vultures to swoop on fresh quarry, were slow to respond. Australia, eager to resolve its colonial complex by having a colony of its own, began to pressure Britain to lay claim to East New Guinea on its behalf. Until 1884 Britain refused. But by then the Germans were showing an interest in the island's north-eastern quarter and, not to be outdone, the British raised their flag in Port Moresby and drew another arbitrary line between themselves and the Germans.

More tenacious colonies were established on the coast and the three European powers intensified their various trading efforts, secured their ports, harried the local population and began experimental plantations. The conquest of New Guinea was complete.

No one looked much further inland than the coastal plains and the low-lying foothills. As far as they could see, the central mountain range was precipitous and too high to be productive. Moreover, it was blocked off on both sides by limestone barriers and giddy gorges, and no one was tempted to waste precious time and money on serious attempts to breach it.

And so, for almost a century after Europeans first established themselves in New Guinea, the most fertile tract of the country – the very area dissected by European pencils – lay locked away behind the clouds. And one million tribal people – the last unknown civilisation on earth – went about their lives cradled, undetected, in the eye of the storm.

CHAPTER 1

Taim Bilong Masta

As the plane took off, the woman in the seat next to mine held my hand as if participating in a seance. She had little stars tattooed on her cheeks and her clothes smelt of woodsmoke. She had trouble fitting a huge string bag into the overhead locker and buckling her seatbelt. When she smiled, her teeth were stained red with betelnut.

After a while, as we circled above the arid hillsides, she released my hand and fell asleep. Beneath us the tiny shadow of our plane wobbled across the desert scrub. Then thorn bush gave way to eucalyptus and slowly eucalyptus became forest, deepening and thickening as the Sogeri foothills led up from the coast through thunderous cloud to the mountains.

We had taken off from Port Moresby, the inevitable sorting office for new arrivals, and not a great introduction to Papua New Guinea. As the country's capital it wears its mantle with conviction; but it is soulless and centreless – a messy South Pacific imitation of LA. There are freeways, highways and dual carriageways, though scarcely fourteen thousand people own cars. And closeted behind the hillsides, between oases of skyrise, are the tell-tale squatter camps of tens of thousands of misguided migrants.

In the expatriate suburbs, bougainvillea and plumbago disguise the paranoia of razor wire and security fences. Alsatians snooze on chains beneath the prefabs; women never walk alone. Gangland violence boils beneath the veneer of a city on the rise.

Though the capital of a now independent nation, Port Moresby bears the hallmarks of a tenacious expatriate community. Some still see it as 'their city', as Australian as Canberra or Cairns. Remarkably, there is little or no racial tension between blacks and their former white *mastas*; but educated nationals resent the fact that it is in Australia's economic interest to keep PNG dependent.

There is a historical context for this resentment. Australia had been churlishly slow to relinquish its hold on PNG in the 1960s and had to be pressured by the United Nations before admitting that the time was ripe for independence. Australians had fought long and hard for control of eastern New Guinea, and they had ousted the Germans from the northern quarter of the island almost as soon as the First World War broke out in Europe. But Australia had to wait until the end of the Second World War before being granted administration of the two former colonies – German and British – under the banner of the Territory of Papua and New Guinea.

By then, with the help of native Papuan foot soldiers, Australia had fought back the Japanese invasion of the country and, in a close call, resisted Japanese attempts to capture Port Moresby via the infamous Kokoda Trail. The Territory had seen some of the fiercest fighting in the South Pacific; and it was with a sense of betrayal that many Australians saw the Papua New Guinean flag, with its scarlet-tailed bird of paradise, flutter aloft for the first time in 1975.

The most incongruous thing about Moresby, apart from its mania for barbies, tinnies and Australian soaps, is its isolation from the rest of PNG. There can be few capital cities in the world that do not connect with any other major town in the country except by sea. Yet nearly a hundred years after its establishment as the capital of British New Guinea, Port Moresby still stands alone. There are as yet no roads beyond the frontier of the Owen Stanley Ranges. There will probably never be railways. The only direct contact Port Moresby has with the Central Highlands is by air.

Most of the people on our internal flight to Goroka in Eastern Highlands Province were nationals, Highlanders with babies and cardboard boxes returning from a visit to the city. There were missionaries too: a couple of Filipino nuns in short grey wimples and a gushing Canadian volunteer wearing Jesus sandals. A German seismologist was plotting with his local counterpart over a tray-table of graphs. On the other side of the curtain, both pilots were unquestionably Australian. The flight attendant with the orange squash and biscuits was coastal Melanesian. Featured on the tail of our Talair aircraft and on our tickets was a tall, befeathered warrior – the company logo. He stood at ease, resting on a spear, unmoved by the diversity of his passengers.

The flight became turbulent but no one seemed alarmed. This was as routine as a bus ride and, given the state of many roads in PNG and the well-publicised incidents of armed hold-ups on the Highlands Highway, considerably less hazardous. Outside, the sunshine of the coast had surrendered to cloud. We were nearing the mighty barriers that had blocked colonial advance for over a century. Limestone crags pierced the forest, shredding

17

mist into the ravines. A great mountain range was ballooning underneath us, its cliff tops within hundreds of feet of the aircraft. The clouds seemed only inches from reach.

At last, an hour or so after take-off, our plane broke through a pass and descended like a dream into the Goroka Valley. This was what had eluded the outside world for so long: a Shangri-la of rich grassland and gushing rivers, one of the most beautiful places on earth.

As we flew lower, a patchwork of fallow and working gardens was revealed – tight mounds of vegetables in pockets of tilled soil and aprons of shade trees protecting coffee crops. There were wisps of smoke from the thatched roofs of villages and from burning grass on the hillsides. The town of Goroka was a sheen of tin roofs packed together around four sides of the airstrip.

It was 1933, the year Hitler became Chancellor and Malcolm Campbell set a new world land-speed record of 272 mph, when news broke that the world's last 'lost' population had been found. The *Sydney Morning Herald* broke the story on November 16:

Stone Age Natives Discovered in New Guinea
Four white men returned to civilisation last month after an exploring trip through the wilds of New Guinea, during which they traversed an area of 4,500 square miles and came into contact with 200,000 natives whose existence had previously been unknown.

The white men, young Australian gold prospectors, had actually breached the Highland fortress three years before but had been reticent about broadcasting their story for fear other prospectors might jump on the bandwagon. They had been encouraged to explore the interior by the discovery of gold in Edie Creek, a tributary of the Bulolo River, only thirty-seven miles from the coast. Hoping to find more gold in the headwaters of the Ramu River, they ventured towards its origins in the Bismarck Ranges, on the border of that great, unexplored blank that then covered twenty-five thousand square miles of the map of New Guinea. The *Sydney Morning Herald* announcement made public their discovery – not of gold, but of hundreds of thousands of people.

It had been assumed by colonialists and cartographers alike that one solid mountain range lay in the centre of New Guinea; instead, the prospectors had discovered two. Jagged and precipitous, they encompassed a chain of fertile, temperate valleys a mere five to six thousand feet above sea level. Far from the hostile, freezing conditions they had expected, the prospectors found a land of perpetual spring, mild and blissfully free of the malaria-carrying mosquito that marred life on the coast. The vast population they came upon thrived in conditions which, as some commentators ventured to suggest, were comparable to a Garden of Eden.

'Garden' at least was an accurate description. The prospectors had been astounded by their first vision of valley agriculture. There were yams, taros and sweet potatoes growing in mounds of tilled earth, and beans and sugar cane in long straight rows. Every garden was drained by ditches and fenced off, with pointed stakes, from domesticated pigs.

The tribesmen, who were naked except for a modest bark-cloth apron and a bushel of leaves over their buttocks, were remarkably strong, healthy and physically fit. The women wore similar loincloths, and long string bags hung down their backs from a knot tied on their heads. Inside the bags, the women carried loads of potatoes and other vegetables pulled from the gardens, and sometimes a baby or a piglet. Many wore shell necklaces and decorations – white cowries or half-moon-shaped pearl shells – evidence that somehow there were native trade routes operating between here and the coast. For the first time, the source of the mysterious bird of paradise skins became apparent: the mountain people all wore fantastic feathers in their hair like strange, mythological bird-men.

Sophisticated though their gardens were, the Highlanders had no knowledge of the artefacts that had revolutionised other civilisations. They hadn't invented the wheel, exploited metal, nor discovered glass. They had no beast of burden and no complicated machinery; they used basic agricultural tools. The quantum leaps of history had passed them by. The Highlanders were living, as far as the colonial administration was concerned, at the beginning of human evolution.

When it breached the mountain wall, the Australian prospecting expedition, with all its technological paraphernalia, had been met by thunderstruck amazement. Crowds engulfed the white men wherever they went, weeping and wailing, laughing and embracing them, stroking their arms and legs, sometimes blowing an eerie tune of greeting on bamboo flutes. Some seemed to believe that the prospectors were spirits returning from the dead, their skin and eyes the colour of ghosts. They reacted with terror, bewildered reverence and, finally, hospitality and welcome.

But all was not well in the garden. The gold-miners noticed that most of the men were battle-scarred, and although (on their first visit at least) they were greeted with open arms, the tribespeople seemed inordinately afraid of their neighbours. The men carried weapons with them at all times – stone axes, bows and arrows, and bone clubs – and when the expedition moved on they would gesticulate wildly as if to warn the prospectors away from enemy territory. The whole valley system, it emerged, was a network of tribal communities at war with each other.

⸻

There were crowds of people beyond the perimeter fence watching our plane when it landed. They watched as we disembarked, like spectators at the changing of the guard admiring a job well executed, on time, familiar. Our arrival advertised the miracle of movement in and out of the mountains.

There were waves and smiles as passengers crossed the tarmac. Men greeted each other with big handshakes and grins and walked off up the high street hand in hand. Fathers affectionately kissed their children and loaded them into the backs of pick-ups. Women chatted in groups, swapping babies and news from the big city. But husbands and wives were reunited with the most perfunctory of greetings, acknowledging each other with an understatement that betrayed a sexual taboo. The woman with the betelnut smile sallied forth up the hill, the weight of her enormous string bag hanging from her head while her husband – dressed in traditional bark apron with leaves over his buttocks – strolled alongside, a diminutive, empty handbag over his shoulder.

The man I was supposed to be meeting was late. I had been given his name by a friend of mine in England who had taught Akunai at Port Moresby University in the early 1970s, when he was a young Highland student new to the outside world. When she heard that I was planning to stop off in Papua New Guinea for a couple of weeks en route to Australia, my friend insisted that I make an effort to contact him.

"Things are changing so fast in the Highlands of PNG," she

said, "faster than anywhere else on earth. Akunai is a remarkable man. In a way he is standing with one foot in the stone age, and the other in the twenty-first century."

So I rang Akunai's sister in Port Moresby, giving details of my arrival and suggesting that Akunai and I might meet. She promised to pass on the word. He would be glad of the company, she said.

As the crowd at the airport dispersed, and even the volunteer had been claimed, I began to think it improbable that a bush telegraph could have survived intact from London to a tiny village in central New Guinea. However, twenty minutes later a Toyota truck whistled round the corner and a smiling, bearded Highlander came forward to shake my hand.

Akunai, now in his mid-thirties and a candidate for the local government elections, was a *big man* in the community, a national with a CV to rival any in the country. He had a Bachelor's degree from Port Moresby University, a Master's in Public Administration and Comparative Politics from Sydney, and several years' travel in Europe, America and Japan under his belt. He was married, now, to a woman from a neighbouring clan and they had a baby daughter. The last few years had been spent 'getting back to grass roots' in the village and reclaiming the respect of his clan after errant years spent abroad.

Even so, he was not what I was expecting. I had imagined something a little less, well, cosmopolitan from a tribesman who had been born barely twenty years after first contact; whose father had been one of the first village leaders converted by missionaries to Christianity; whose uncle was a famous local warrior who had eaten his due of human flesh. This dapper young man in sports shirt and porkpie hat barely tallied with my preconceptions of a New Guinea Highlander. He had a kind, intelligent face and eyes that twinkled with amusement. Again, not the kind of refinement I had bargained for.

"Welcome to Goroka," he was saying as he took my bags. "It will be good to talk to someone from outside PNG. It can seem very cut off up here, even with all our mod cons." 'Mod cons', I learnt, included satellite TV, the latest telephone communications system and ubiquitous computer technology.

I had arrived, he told me, at a busy time of year. Village coffee crops were ripening and Akunai was campaigning for local elections. But he was eager to sidestep the chaos for a while and suggested we go straight to the village and 'get down to some good stories'.

We loaded my rucksack into the back of the truck, along with empty flour bags he had just picked up for his coffee pickers, and boxes of sugar, tinned fish and rice. "That's just to keep them going," he said, starting the truck. "When they've finished picking I'll give them a whole calf and a crate of beer. But if I pay them now, we'll have a wholesale *pati* on our hands and no coffee berries to show for it."

Akunai spoke with a soft voice and just the hint of an accent that made the Australian overtones almost exotic. He waved to some white businessmen as we passed by the Agricultural Bank in the centre of town.

"It's the crazy season now," he said, almost apologetically, "the 'coffee flush'. Everyone's buying things – clothes, cars, beer. There's more people drunk, more accidents, more hold-ups at this time of year. Everyone goes crazy until the money runs out again. You'll see some pretty wild behaviour while you're here."

As if to prove his point, we slowed down to avoid a scuffle that had broken out in the forecourt of a supermarket. A couple

23

of local women tried to flag us down for a lift but Akunai drove past them. He noticed my surprise.

"We can't pick anyone up," he explained, "unless they're a *wantok*. The claims for compensation would be too big if we injured them in an accident. The way things are at the moment, it might even spark a clan war."

"*Wantok*?" I queried, and received my first, crucial lesson in the perplexities of ritual *payback*.

Traditionally, there is no such thing as an accident in PNG. There is always someone connected to the incident who can be blamed for it. If a man jumps off a speeding truck and breaks his leg, it is not his fault. It is the truck owner's fault, or the driver's fault, or even the fault of the person who took him to hospital. The compensation fiascos that occur in the United States have nothing on the principles of liability in Papua New Guinea. It makes for the most complicated and vigorously enforced insurance scheme in the world.

The injured party has the right to claim compensation from the person he believes was responsible for the accident. Usually he will ask for an enormous sum – anything from a few hundred kina (the equivalent of hundreds of Australian dollars), crates of beer and a few pigs (worth anything up to six hundred kina each in the Highlands) to a new Nissan truck.

This is where the *wantok* system kicks in. A *wantok* – literally 'one talk' – is any person who speaks your mother tongue: a member of your family or clan. In PNG the number of people speaking any one traditional language is remarkably small. This reflects both the geography of the country and the marked self-sufficiency of tribal groups. There are roughly seven hundred and fifty distinct and mutually unintelligible languages in PNG – one-third of the world's total.

Within the system, if someone claims *payback* from you, your *wantoks* can be depended upon to come to your aid, lending you the necessary amounts for compensation. They may already be indebted to you for past service in a similar case; but in any event, the practice serves to bond the family and bolster clan loyalty. Likewise, if the injured party has trouble exacting payment, his *wantoks* will rally round to threaten or cajole the 'guilty' party into paying. Not surprisingly, these negotiations are fraught with disagreement and the two sides often go to war over the matter.

Usually the conflict is little more than a ritualistic battle, both sides withdrawing when a certain number of men have been wounded or killed. But the pendulum may still be in motion, one side aggrieved that they have lost more men than the other, and the cycle of *payback* continues. The status quo amongst Highland clans has depended throughout history on an uneasy succession of allegiances, animosity and indebtedness handed down from one generation to another. Tribesmen today are battling out grievances that originated hundreds of years ago.

"Of course, the police are supposed to clamp down on the old system of *payback* – try and introduce some form of modern justice," said Akunai. "But it's very difficult. If you're a policeman and your *wantok* is thrown in jail for killing one of your enemies, you are obliged to help him. Prisoners often escape from jail because their guards are looking the other way."

Translated into contemporary life, the *wantok* system thrives like a virus. There are more chances of having an accident in the modern world: there are roads, cars, trucks and many more people; there are planes and modern machinery, alcohol and guns. In town, in particular, the odds are uncomfortably stacked against you.

So it was with some relief that we left the madding crowds

25

behind and headed east along the deserted Highlands Highway towards Akunai's village. The bustle of the Eastern Highland's capital gave way to the suburbs: a motley collection of tradestores and clapboard houses. Here and there a tin sign advertised Fanta or Pepsi or Rothmans. Some were in English, others in unvarnished pidgin.

We passed a hand-painted billboard with tribal warriors drinking from familiar glass bottles. The slogan read in pidgin 'Coke *tasol*', meaning literally 'Coke – That's all'; a more modest image than the great 'Coke is it' campaign intended.

Pidgin is an easy language, I discovered, even for a first-time visitor. It is the lingua franca of the country, an ingenious local invention that bridges the divides between PNG's seven hundred and fifty indigenous languages, as well as the linguistic task forces of German and English. Pidgin is the ultimate happy medium. It tends to say in words of one syllable what the European would elaborate into polysyllabic technobabble. It cuts the crap. Which is one reason why it was condemned by the colonials, and still is by some ex-pats, as 'baby talk'.

Tok pisin, as it calls itself, has no unnecessary articles, pronouns and prepositions, no plural nouns, no confusing verb tenses, and it is phonetically spelt. There are only thirteen hundred words to remember, compared to six thousand in English, and the more unusual words are logical compounds of the basic nouns: a thumb is *nambawan pinga*; a toe is *pinga bilong fut*.

But the language really comes into its own when it describes the trappings of western culture – the technology by which colonial *mastas* tried to assert their superiority. A refrigerator when first encountered by a Papua New Guinean was simply an icebox (as it is in the States), or a *bokis ais*; a generator became a *masin bilong mekim lektrik*; a towel was obviously a *lap-lap* (or loincloth) *bilong waswas*; and disinfectant, that reassuring western panacea, just *marasin bilong klinim sua*. Even figureheads like the Pope were inadvertently put in their place when described as *nambawan Jisas man*. And Prince Charles, who attended the country's independence celebrations, was pidgin-holed (to coin a phrase) as *nambawan pikinini bilong Misis Kwin*.

Pidgin demystified the modern world, which is probably why the modern world – and the *Jacaranda Dictionary of Melanesian Pidgin*, reluctantly compiled by the missionary Reverend Francis Mihalic – considered its use demeaning.

Nowadays, though, gadgets are known more commonly by a tradename or simply spelt phonetically. When ex-pats insist that a 'piano' in pidgin is *wan bikpela bokis insait i gat planti teet olsem sark na taim missus i hitim na kikim bikpela bokis i singaut tumas* (a big box with lots of teeth inside like a shark which makes a lot of noise when the lady of the house hits it and kicks it) or, indeed, that a *helikopta* is still known as a *Mix-Master bilong Jisas*, they are stretching the point.

Beyond Goroka the Highlands Highway stretched seamlessly into the distance. Around us rolled bare hills, as expansive as the Highlands of Scotland but without the heather. Smoke drifted from the hillsides where villagers were burning *kunai* grass to recharge the soil for new gardens. In the occasional lay-by, young boys sat at spindly wooden stalls offering the passing motorist a single cabbage or a neat pyramid of tomatoes. Women, busy crocheting their string bags, or *bilums*, awaited custom, legs outstretched on the ground, with cucumbers, sweetcorn and spring greens spread before them on blue plastic, like a picnic. There was no urgency here, only the take-it-or-leave-it insouciance of a people as yet unpressed by the austerities that come with overpopulation.

There were, however, an inordinate number of pigs about the place. There were big ones and small ones; wiry, athletic ones and fat, full-bellied mamas that idled along by the side of the road. They were not naked and pink like their factory-farmed cousins back home, but bristly and dark, and they roamed at large as self-assured and independent as domestic cats or dogs. In the Highlands of New Guinea, pigs represent wealth and social standing. In village business, a transaction may be conducted just as easily with a payment of pigs as with modern currency. The value of a pig has little bearing on its actual market price. It represents something more than the sum of skin, bone and bristle, or the potential for sausage meat. Entrepreneurs have tried, and failed, to farm pigs in the Highlands and flood the market. So exclusive is the place of the pig in Highland culture that cheap pigs paid for in cash were anathema to the tribal way of thinking, and the modern pig producers were ignored.

Pigs from Asia were probably introduced to the island about ten thousand years ago and were domesticated soon after the first people settled and started gardening in the Highland valleys about a thousand years later. They never looked back. They became the responsibility of the women, who love and pet them, scratch and de-tick them, feed them scraps and sleep with them in their huts at night. Sometimes they are given names and come stampeding through the undergrowth for a tit-bit when called. When a garden is harvested they are turned loose to dig up the remaining tubers, simultaneously fertilising and tilling the soil for the next crop.

Women have been known to suckle orphan piglets or the runts of a litter – a practice the early missionaries found particularly abhorrent. Unable, however, to eradicate it, the missionaries came to a compromise: the women could suckle a piglet on the left breast, as it was on the side of the Devil, but they must reserve the right breast, belonging to God, for their children.

Akunai had the storytelling talents of a Highlands Homer. As he warmed to the role of raconteur and the chance to captivate a newcomer, Akunai's stories gathered momentum. His was a tale unique in its particulars and yet at heart common to every Highlander of his age. We drove on through the open Goroka landscape while Akunai's descriptions evoked a time only thirty years before when there were fewer people; when there were forests on the hillsides, spiky boundary fences demarking village territory, and only the occasional glinting tin roof of a church or government tradestore. The villagers we passed would not have been wearing *sekonhan klos* from Australia, but bark cloth and tanget leaves; the tarmac highway we were travelling along would have been little more than a bumpy dirt track, one of a myriad that formed the valley network. And it would have taken us half a day to get this far from Goroka.

Akunai grew up at Tarabo on the Okapa mission station, which was one of the first in the valley; his father was a Christian convert who was trained by the Lutherans as an evangelist. Akunai was the fifth of eight children spun early into the orbit of the white man through their father's calling. When he was eight or nine years old (like most Highlanders his age, there is no official record of his birthday), he was sent with other boys from the Lutheran mission to an American missionary school forty miles away in Asaro near Goroka.

The two-day journey to school at the beginning of each term terrified Akunai and his friends. They had to cross territory belonging to enemy clans, and creep through thick forests inhabited by spirits. They ran as much as possible, snatching a few wary hours' sleep in the bushes only when they were too exhausted to continue.

The Asaro Lutheran High School presented different fears. The missionaries – mostly worthy women in their thirties and forties – were kind and maternal, but their behaviour was bizarre. The principle they most insisted upon – one that Akunai began to realise consumed most white people – was that 'Cleanliness is next to Godliness'. For a native-born Highlander this notion was unthinkable. Where did it leave the rest of the clan, Akunai thought, living as they must in the unavoidable dirt of the village?

Nonetheless, Akunai and his friends were bathed every week and wrestled into western clothes – the money for which they would earn washing dishes and cleaning houses. Their shirts felt scratchy and tight under the arms; their trousers restricted the energetic scampering they could enjoy back at home. One of the pleasures of the end of term was to be able to strip off once again and revert to the freedom of a neat sheaf of tanget leaves.

One of the habits Akunai found impossible to adopt was blowing his nose into a white cotton *hankisip*. He couldn't understand what was so special about snot that you would want to save it, and so he would flick his on the ground with his fingers like the rest of the boys. Perhaps the missionaries had a use for their snot that he didn't know about.

Despite their vagaries, Akunai grew fond of the Americans. He trusted them and did his best to please them, learning to bake banana cake for their tea by mimicking their every movement in the kitchen. Unlike the villagers, who ate a modest repast of greens and sweet potatoes once a day, with cold taro and sweet potato for breakfast, the missionaries ate a phenomenal amount, packing away three large meals every day, with coffee and cake in between.

Akunai was eager and quick to learn, picking up the rudiments of piano-playing along with his regular schooling. He painted watercolours which he sold to teachers and other white people who visited the school. Soon his ability eclipsed the rest of his class.

In the mid-1960s, when Akunai was in his early teens, the Australian administration, under United Nations instructions, established a special school outside Port Moresby to groom a new generation of nationals for self-government. Akunai was one of three from the Eastern Highlands – and among the top five percent of all high-school students in the country – chosen to attend.

The day Akunai was due to leave for the capital was perhaps the most frightening of his life. Once, when he was a young boy, he had driven down to the coast with his uncle, along the brand-new Highlands Highway, and the sight of that great, blue expanse of sea had horrified him. At first he had thought that the sea was an area of the Markham Valley that had been burnt out by bush fires, until, at closer range, he recognised it as a gigantic, moving lake. But the horror of that adventure was nothing compared to the prospect of taking to the skies in an airplane.

His whole family had assembled on the grass airstrip to see him off, weeping and wailing as if he were already dead. Trembling with fear, he and the two other boys climbed the steps of the old Fokker Friendship plane expecting never to see the Highlands again. As they taxied down the runway all three were too frightened to look through the windows and wave goodbye. They huddled in their seats, eyes fixed rigidly on the floor.

Four hours and several sick bags later, they touched down in Port Moresby. They were told to get off the plane, and as they reached the door were struck full in the face by a dry blanket of suffocating hot air. There was a numbness in their ears as if their eardrums had been blown out, and their legs shook like the tails of newborn puppies.

The airport buildings, then not even a terminal to speak of, were like nothing they had seen before. There were more people milling around the arrivals hall than Akunai had ever imagined existed. Everything he saw and heard – the unfamiliar faces of the coastal people, the sound of car horns, the smell of take-away food, the abrasion of bursting sunlight – was outlandish and frightening. The three boys wandered about at a loss, in shock.

Sogeri School was a twenty-eight-mile drive from Port Moresby. It was in the foothills of the Owen Stanley Ranges, so the air was cooler and the hills smacked vaguely, even spitefully, of home. It dawned on the boys that the Goroka Valley was barred from them, a lifetime away behind the clouds.

For the first few months the boys were miserably homesick. The school was run with military precision and the discipline of the rod. Every ratchet of the day was heralded by the ringing of bells. The boys were taught to fold hospital corners on their beds and polish their shoes until their faces gleamed back at them.

Akunai clung to his Highland fellows like a cuscus to the branches of a tree. Though the teachers tried to persuade them to make other friends, Akunai couldn't trust boys who came from who knew where. He was humiliated by having to share his textbook with a girl and, speechless with embarrassment, refused to answer questions in front of her in class.

In the Highlands he had grown accustomed to the occasional white face, but at Sogeri the teachers and groundstaff, even the cleaners and cooks, were white. Anxious and confused, Akunai found himself eating off plates washed by a white person. It was as if the world had capsized. Clearly, some of the older teachers felt the same, railing at the indecorum of treating dirty *pikininis* with kid gloves.

The blue skies of my arrival were now threatened by storm clouds, the volatile mountain atmosphere responding to an afternoon drop in air temperature. Along the road, children were carrying fronds of pitpit, a kind of multipurpose bamboo used for building, eating and killing – its slender, straight stems were fashioned by their fathers into perfectly weighted Highland arrows used for hunting. As we passed the children, they dropped the pitpit fronds and ran after us, shouting and cheering and loosing imaginary bows in our direction, as instinctively as western children might take pot-shots at a passing car with make-believe pistols.

On the right, as we cleared another bend, the distinctive peak of Mt Michael materialised in the distance.

"That's where the Okapa mission station is," said Akunai, "where we grew up. I used to think that was where our family came from until we moved back to our village. Then I realised that all along we'd come from somewhere else."

It had been a disconcerting revelation. His elder brothers and sisters could remember their village, but Akunai had invested all his early loyalties in another clan's land. He felt dislocated somehow, cheated of one of the fundamental birthrights of a Highlander. He clearly felt uneasy discussing it. The past was firm ground but he had ventured by implication into the shifting sands of the present. He switched blithely back onto an anecdotal track.

"Okapa is where they have 'Kuru' – the Laughing Disease," he recalled with relish. "I remember as a child seeing women brought into the hospital on the mission station, and then only days later seeing them carried out to be buried. They used to laugh all the time until they died, screaming and shouting and shaking, and crawling around the floor like pigs. We were frightened of them as kids – we thought the spirits had possessed them."

There were still well-publicised cases of Kuru in Okapa. I had read about one only recently in, of all things, the *Farmer's Weekly*. Missionaries and the media loved to dwell on the grue-some effects of the disease and hypothesise about the affliction as a visitation of the Devil – divine retribution for transgressing one of God's most sacred unwritten commandments: 'Thou shalt not eat another human being'. For the Laughing Disease is only transmitted by eating the brains of an infected person – a practice ritually performed by certain clans in the Okapa district. The virus, which can lie deceptively dormant for years and concen-trates itself in the brain, eventually attacks the central nervous system and sends the victim mad – like Mad Cow Disease among European cattle which have been fed cattle offal.

Christianity and moral outrage on the part of the colonial establishment had done much to eradicate the ritual in Okapa (the present victims had almost certainly contracted the disease in childhood, around the time Akunai was living on the station). But local villagers still felt ambiguous about the practice, blaming their present misfortunes on the betrayal of ancient tradition. They found it confusing, Akunai said, that the Christians should be so intolerant of cannibalism in Okapa when they ate the flesh and drank the blood of their own kind every Sunday.

"There's still a lot of sorcery around Okapa," said Akunai. "People there still hold strong beliefs in the spirits and the ancestors. Even people who have converted believe in the old ways as well as the new. If someone gets sick, they'll most likely go to hospital *and* get the local spirit man to work some magic." He chuckled. "That's how it works in the Highlands. We try and get the best of both worlds."

We were nearing the turn-off to Akunai's village and on either side of the road now, shaded by spindly casuarinas, were small plots of coffee trees, their branches thick with ripening berries. They still had a smattering of white blossom, and the scent breezed through the windows as sweet and exotic as jasmine or frangipani. On the verge, women were sitting beside petrol cans full of red berries, the first of this year's crop, waiting for the commercial coffee trucks to pick up the harvest for processing.

Ever since the German *mastas* introduced coffee to the Highlands in the 1940s and discovered the ideal climate and soil for growing the arabica bean, the plant has played a vital part in the Highlands' economy. There were endless stories around Goroka about how it all began.

Local legend had it that the *mastas'* cookboys were quick to recognise the potential of the crop and stole cuttings to plant in their own gardens. When the Korean War, combined with a drought in Brazil, pushed up world coffee prices in 1953, these unsuspecting villagers – with only six years' experience of paper money – became kina millionaires.

It was a story which appealed greatly to the mischievous Highland spirit: support for the underdog who triumphs over wealthy colonials. Most of it, though, was wishful thinking and the *kukboi* turned coffee baron turns up in a hundred different stories. In fact, only one Highlander is known to have made a killing from coffee. Khasanwaho Baito Herio had been a servant to one of the early Australian explorers. He earned so much money from copying his *masta's* coffee ventures that he became the first Highlander to own a Land Rover.

As a coffee-grower himself, however, Akunai was all too aware of an innate hostility to the product amongst villagers. They were instinctively reluctant to trust any crop that took three years to mature, that required constant attention and was inedible at the end of it. While European settlers were snapping up land around Goroka and making their fortunes, villagers had to be actively persuaded by Australian government officers to plant coffee.

It had taken independence and a severe frost in Brazil for Highlanders to finally appreciate coffee. In 1975 prices soared and suddenly everyone started planting. Now, over seventy per cent of PNG's coffee is grown by locals in tiny village plots. The emblem of Eastern Highlands Province has the legendary local spirit, Nokondi – harbinger of good fortune and healthy crops, and guardian against hostile tribes – brandishing a coffee branch.

Shortly after the local coffee capital of Henganofi, and several miles short of Kainantu, Akunai slowed the truck to a halt in a lay-by.

"This is where we turn off," he announced, and pointed the front of the truck over the verge at a forty-five-degree angle towards the gully below. The track we appeared to be after was little more than a crack in the ground, pitted with crevices from run-off. We lurched and rocked from side to side, careering towards the river at the bottom in order to gather enough speed to climb out the other side. As the truck tore through the water, tyres spinning on gravel, Akunai deftly switched to four-wheel drive and tipped us up and over the other side.

"The villagers made this road themselves," he shouted above the screeching engine. "It took twenty people from three different villages to do it. They dug it out with spades – all five and a half miles of it. Took three weeks."

"Handmade," he added, triumphantly.

Over the brow of the ridge up ahead, a panorama of rolling hills came into view. In the distance, nestling on the saddle between limestone peaks, swathed in the last vestiges of forest, was Akunai's village.

CHAPTER 2

Taim God i Kamap Long Isten Hailans

It was musty and still inside Akunai's hut – the empty darkness of visits repeatedly postponed. This was a new house, like most in his village. The old round huts with their thatch raised in twin peaks had been outdone by modern compromise. Gone, too, were the distinctive tufts of grass – one from the owner's patch, one from a neighbouring area – that would whisper to each other from the roof peaks during the night. Now Akunai had no way of knowing his neighbour's secrets.

Most houses in the village were rectangular like this one, partitioned into sleeping quarters. The nine-thousand-foot altitude no longer meant huddling together against the embers, kippered by smoke while you slept. Only the older people still wheezed and coughed on the floor by the fire, reluctant to give up the warmth of the old ways for an extra blanket and easier lungs. There were now a few corrugated-iron roofs in the village, although not over this house. The impermanence of thatch was still, on balance, preferable to the hammering rat-tat-tat-tat of the rain and the baking effect of the sun.

Akunai's house was set a little apart from the village, in its own compound, and while he was away it was locked with an over-stated padlock. Privacy was a guarded privilege and one that singled out Akunai as a villager with outside pretensions.

With the crackle of wood and the rumble of water in the kettle, a sense of occupancy slowly reasserted itself. The stale, fallow air dispersed through cracks in the pitpit walls. Out of the darkness, an old woman crept silently over the threshold to place several sweet potatoes, still warm, on a tin plate by the fire. Akunai nodded and shook her hand.

Barely able to contain her curiosity she sat down on the grass mat beside me, proffering a leathery handshake and an ecstatic smile. Gently, like a child with a wild animal, she stroked the white skin of my arm and fingered my hair. Akunai offered her a few words by way of explanation in Kamano, the language of their clan. She beamed at me in wonder and continued stroking. After a while, as unceremoniously as she had entered, she slipped away.

When Akunai's brother Baito entered the hut, their greeting was without ceremony. They relaxed readily into *tok ples* – literally 'talk place', their local language – to exchange the latest news. Baito was probably only eight years older than Akunai, but as eldest son he had been most aware of their father's conversion from village *big man* to Lutheran minister. He had stayed most of his adult life in the village, speaking no English and only fair pidgin, opting for the tradition of two wives and a wealth of pigs instead of the dubious benefits of monogamy and paper money.

He cut a prepossessing figure, ladling spoonful after spoonful of sugar into his tea, and stirring thoughtfully, deliberately. He was not tall, but trim and strong, neatly dressed in jeans and a faded, red-checked shirt with rolled-up sleeves. His hair was greying at the temples, giving him the distinguished air of an elder statesman. His hands lay relaxed in his lap as he nodded quietly to Akunai's conversation. There was a stillness about him, like a perfectly weighted plumb-line, a calm contrast to his younger brother. Akunai fidgeted as he spoke, trying to get comfortable on the beaten floor. He looked for support; his back had suffered once too often from the handmade road to his village. He helped himself to an SP – a bottle of South Pacific beer with a bird of paradise on the label – and handed me another from the box of overnight supplies.

When Baito began to speak, his voice was low and continuous like a shaman reciting a mantra. He stopped at lay-bys in his story to take a slurp of tea and allow Akunai time to translate. The story he told had been cobbled and reworked, tempered and proven, enlivening the long village evenings for decades, until it buoyed up the teller and his listeners in some fabulous ark against the capricious open sea.

Long taim bifo, Baito began, when their father, Sabumei, was young, their village was hidden in a mighty forest. The place was alive with the sound of birds calling to each other. Birds of paradise danced in the treetops and men made glorious head-dresses from their feathers. Since the age of the ancestors men had done this, because they had made an agreement with the birds. In the beginning they had been offered a choice: immortality or mortality; the way of the snake, which sheds its skin and is born again, or the way of the birds and the joy of flight. The ancestors chose flight, and the birds freely lent their wings so that man might know how it feels to fly. And ever after, when their sons and grandsons held *sing-sings*, the Highlanders would dress up in feathers and dance and sing like the birds.

There were not only birds in the forest at that time. There was plenty of game – wild pigs, cassowaries, tree kangaroos and cuscus. But the forest was also a frightening place. It shielded enemies, and villagers were afraid to wander too far, or neighbouring tribes hiding in wait might catch and kill them. There were constant battles. Sometimes there was no time to rebuild the razed village and so villagers would live in temporary shelters under trees and tend their gardens under armed guard.

The spirits, too, had made the forest their home. Often you would hear their voices calling from the caves, or even see them, leaping and running through the trees. There was one place, a clearing in the forest, where nothing ever grew – not even grass – and no leaf ever fell. It was a sacred spot, where the spirits held their *sing-sings*, dancing on the earthen floor, beating their great *kundu* drums and chanting sacred songs. When villagers heard drums thumping in the night, they would go to the clearing to find things that the spirits had left behind, forgetful in the excitement of their *sing-sing*. There were spirits of a different kind in the trees. Some of the great old trees were powerful and strong. You could lose your hearing or your eyesight if you walked between them in certain places. People were scared of the shapes they made and the strange, creaking, rustling noises that surrounded them.

There were lakes too – dark, eerie, bottomless lakes. One lake next to the village was a favourite with the spirits. No one ever went too close, although sometimes they would watch the lake from a distance, to see if they could catch a glimpse of the ancestors going down to bathe.

"When the white man came," said Baito, "everything began to change. He cut down the forest from village to village so he could ride his horses. Then the birds and the spirits moved away. We no longer heard their *kundu* drums in the night, or their voices. Then the grass began to grow in their sacred clearing and we knew they had gone. The forest fell silent and the people were no longer so scared of it. They, too, started cutting down trees to make more gardens, and to help the white man make roads and fell timber for his churches. Soon even the lakes drained away.

"We used to say that the spirits came from this tall mountain, Mt Sunavi, in the valley – you can see it from the hills over there, near Henganofi. On clear days it stands out like the steeple of a church. Only men were allowed to look at it directly; women and children had to avert their eyes out of respect to the ancestors. When the white man came and started building steeples in the image of the sacred mountain, and talking about the souls of the dead and the Holy Ghost, we realised that the spirits were making different homes for themselves and that these white men were probably our ancestors who had come back to visit us."

The villagers knew that strangers were on their way towards them. News seared across the ranges like bushfire, alerting the *big men* to the strange white spirits coming up the valleys. The strangers did not walk but sat on gigantic animals. They came with a new breed of people – the Melanesian evangelists they had already converted on the coast. Often these evangelists would be sent ahead to prepare the villagers for the arrival of the white man. They would bring with them one or two people from a nearby village who could speak the next-door language and so explain what was going on. But the evangelists seemed strange to the Highlanders. They looked familiar – they had the same faces, the same skin – but they were already with the white man. They washed, cut their hair and dressed in clothes – T-shirts and lap-laps. They smelt different and the villagers were scared. They thought they were dead people.

But the evangelists picked off some leaves, a traditional

gesture, and waved them, shouting, "We are people. You don't have to run away." They begged the villagers to sit down so they could talk to them.

Slowly the villagers became curious and stood closer. When one of the evangelists touched someone, they thought he must be a dead relative returned to make friends. Finally, the people started listening to their speeches about peace and friendship, about God and the Holy Spirit, and some of them, including a young man called Sabumei, decided to go with the evangelists to the mission station up near Kainantu, to see the white man and find out what it was all about. The evangelists gave them T-shirts and lap-laps to wear and they went away looking just like the Christians.

For Sabumei, the evangelists' message of peace signalled a potential end to the tit-for-tat warfare that had intensified in the valley over recent years. The Christians had come at just the right time. He saw in them a chance to call a truce with his enemies; a chance for his clan to build permanent homes instead of running from smoking shelters back into the trees; a chance to see their crops grow to fruition in gardens they would dig in the good valley soil, instead of scavenging for remains after the enemies' pigs had ravaged their *kaukau*. But most of all, he saw the chance to live without fear.

The Lutherans had actually reached the Highlands several years before the Australian gold-miners. But they, too, had kept their lips sealed. Publicity would have alerted other fishers of men – the Baptists, Anglicans, Wesleyans, American Seventh Day Adventists, Australian Methodists, English Congregationalists or, worst of all, the French Roman Catholics – to

43

the biggest catch left to the modern missionary.

They had come from Finschhafen on the east coast, headquarters for the Lutheran Mission in German New Guinea, and directed by their indomitable leader, Johann Flierl, had made their first assault on the mountains in 1919 by scaling the Kratke Range – a 3300-foot wall rising straight out of the Markham Valley. By 1930, the year the Australians launched their first expedition, Johann's eldest son, Willie Flierl, and his companion, Reverend Bergmann, were exploring as far as Onerunka and the hills south-west of the Kainantu Valley where Akunai's village lay.

The Australian expedition heralded an onslaught of traders and independent gold-miners. The first government patrol post was set up at Kainantu in 1932, and in 1933 the first Highland airstrip was built at Lapumpa, just outside Kainantu. Missionaries from other denominations were quick to make up for lost time. After fourteen years as the sole agent for God in the Highlands, the Lutherans had to stand by and watch Seventh Day Adventists – Americans at that – found their first Highland station in Kainantu, while the Roman Catholics cornered territory way to the west in Simbu Province.

By the 1940s the race was on. The Lutherans were setting their sights on areas further west towards Mt Hagen and beyond, recruiting and training local evangelists, setting up new camps and mapping out sites for the construction of churches. Then suddenly, like a thunderbolt from heaven, disaster struck. The Second World War broke out and all Germans were recalled to Finschhafen and sent home. The missionaries, ever optimistic, were eager to salvage something of their work and hurriedly arranged to take their Highland evangelists back to Germany with them for further training. Akunai's father and his brother were all set to leave when the local Australian *kiap* intervened and instructed the Germans to go it alone. Akunai's father and uncle returned to their village, took off their lap-laps and T-shirts and resumed village life almost as if nothing had happened.

It was not until after the war, when the Germans, undaunted, returned to regroup the faithful, that Akunai's father became well and truly hooked. He was baptised, and learnt from the second wave of Lutheran ministers the art of preaching to the unconverted; eventually, he set off on crusading missions of his own.

"It was on one of these early 'crusades'," said Baito, "that our father first met our mother, Ato. She was betrothed to a man from a village near Henganofi. He had already paid her bride price with pigs and kina shells, but suddenly he fell sick and took to his bed. Our father was taken to him to work some Christian magic.

"All he could do was give him the last rites. But the man was so pleased that he bequeathed our father his future wife. When the man died, our father went to Tanafa, a village in the Faure region, to claim Ato for himself, according to tribal custom, and brought her back to his home. On the way back, our mother saw an angel flying over the village, and she knew her husband had been chosen specially by the new God."

When the couple arrived back, everyone was surprised that Sabumei had chosen only one wife, because he was a handsome, impressive man. But Sabumei insisted: "This is according to the laws of the Christian God," and told everyone they should try and stick to one wife.

Baito poured us all some tea, his mind deep in the past.

"I was about four years old when I saw my first white man," he said at last. Akunai smiled as he again translated, anticipating one of his favourite stories.

45

"Our father was taking me and a few other young boys down to Kainantu," Baito said, "with baskets full of tree tomatoes to sell to the local *kiap*. Suddenly there was a great rustling and stamping beside us in the long *kunai* grass. I was terrified. My heart was pounding like a drum. I didn't know what it could be.

"I looked up and saw a great big animal – far bigger than any pig I had ever seen. It was sweating and making noises from its nose. All us young boys ran for our lives and our father was calling and calling us to come back. But we hid and waited until the monster was a long, long way ahead before we dared come out.

"And our father said, 'It's all right, it's only a horse. White men ride on their backs so they don't get tired'. But we didn't care – we just didn't want to see another one.

"Then we went down to the *haus kiap* at Kainantu to wait for the white man to come out. We sat by our baskets in the shade of a tree, and us boys didn't know what to expect. Suddenly the white man came out on the veranda.

"When I saw him," said Baito with glee, "I screamed with terror and hid under my father's leg. I was shouting that I didn't want to come out, holding on to his leg and sweating all over. When he came closer, we smelt the white man's smell of soap or whatever and me and the other kids were so scared we almost wet ourselves."

By now Baito and Akunai were laughing so much they could hardly speak. They wiped tears from their eyes and shook their heads at the folly of it all.

"When people started going to town more often, they would see the white man and eventually even the kids got used to him," said Baito.

In the following years, Sabumei spent more and more time away from the village, spreading the word of the white man and, as his eldest sons grew strong enough to travel, occasionally taking them with him. Baito remembered how nerve-racking it was to walk into a strange new village in the wake of his zealous and determined father, how acutely conscious he was of his western clothes and how anxious about the reception awaiting him.

Sabumei was always calm and confident and it was never long before the villagers put their trust in him and sat down to listen to him talk. He would explain about the white man and his different ways: he would say that the missionaries came with a message of peace and brotherhood; that the village people should stop fighting and stealing other people's women; that they could build good, strong homes out in the open. He showed them how to lay out their houses in rows and live as the Europeans did, in a 'civilised' community.

To demonstrate that this was a message of peace, Sabumei would invite each village's enemies to share in a *mumu* – a pig feast cooked in traditional earth ovens. Everyone thought he was mad; this kind of behaviour was courting disaster. Baito, in particular, was terrified. The enemy tribe would approach the village as if walking into a trap. Dressed in all their finery, wearing *bilas*, paint on their faces and long, colourful feathers trembling in their head-dresses, they were tense and suspicious.

Both sides would carry bows and arrows, and for hour upon hour the guests would hover on the outskirts of the village. Finally, Sabumei would entice them, step by step, into the village and invite them to sit down at the ovens to receive their food. At first they would be suspicious of poison and refuse to eat. Baito would watch them like an eagle, waiting for any false move or misunderstanding that might fire up an argument. He was always ready to run for cover and didn't relax a muscle until the *mumu* was over and the guests had gone home.

Slowly, a combination of religious choice and legal enforcement brought a strange, hesitant sort of peace to the Eastern Highlands. By the time Sabumei had been posted to the mission station in the Okapa region, tribal battles had become the exception rather than the rule. And by the time Akunai was old enough to travel with his father, there were few villages unacquainted with the white man or untouched by the word of God. Sabumei's missions into the bush began to take the form of a routine inspection rather than an evangelising crusade.

On these occasions, Akunai used to trail behind his father carrying a wind-up gramophone. The other villagers had seen nothing like this before and were unfailingly impressed. The Lutherans had given Sabumei a box of seventy-eights – sermons recorded by a white preacher and songs from local villages. Akunai would set the gramophone on the ground and sit beside it, waiting for his cue.

"My eyes would get sleepy when our father started preaching and sometimes it was difficult to stay awake. I would have to stare at the trees or the bushes, searching for something to keep me occupied.

"Then suddenly he would tell me to wind up the gramophone and I'd throw on a record and turn the handle. If I wound it too fast, the sound would come out like birds twittering; if my arm grew tired, the trumpet would start groaning – 'waaaaa-waaaaaa-waaaaa' – and I'd have to try to keep going until the end of the record."

Sometimes Akunai would take the gramophone to a graveside and play a mourning song while Sabumei buried the dead. No longer frightened of the spirits, people now wanted to bury their dead near their houses, and not in some remote part of the forest as before.

When a village was ready to be baptised, the villagers would send for Sabumei and the white missionary, and prepare themselves for the *baptaisim* ceremony. It was always a big occasion, with several villages taking part over two or three days. They would light a big bonfire, and the white missionary would say that before the people could be baptised into the House of the Lord, they must burn every instrument of war and sorcery. The people would come with their ceremonial bows and arrows, spears and painted shields, their great feathered head-dresses that made them like birds, and their paraphernalia of magic bark and leaves. They would line up in front of the priest and swear in turn before the Holy Father to renounce the Devil and all his ways, never to dance again at *sing-sings*, and never again to go to war. Then one by one they would throw all the trappings of their former life into the fire and file down to the river in their new white lap-laps to be born again.

"The way of the early missionaries was wrong," said Akunai. "They saw things only in black and white. Everything that was traditional was bad and there was no place for it in the new Christian way of life."

Then a mischievous look came into his eyes.

"But that didn't mean we burnt everything when they asked us to. Often people would bring only their worst bows and arrows, and pieces of bark and so-called sorcery materials that didn't mean anything. People weren't stupid – they wanted to take advantage of the white man and go back to the old ways when they chose.

"Look around you. We still have our bows and arrows, our traditional head-dresses, our songs. I don't think many traditions have died out. They may have been adapted to modern times, but they're too ingrained to be wiped out just like that.

"People still believe in magic above everything else. Anything that happens in the village – accidents, arguments, fights – it's all explained by *sanguma*. If someone dies and the doctor says he died of liver failure, the villagers simply don't believe it. Their natural instinct is to look to the ancestors for an explanation. Christianity has been good to us. It has brought us health and peace, but people still live by their traditions."

The tribal spirit of *long taim bifo* was alive and kicking and playing havoc with local government reform. If the outside world had imposed its authority on the Highlands over the past fifty years, it had done so under stress. Westernisation, so far, was a veneer on the bedrock of local custom. Compensation claims and tribal fighting put paid to western ways of going about things, but in many cases technology in PNG, thanks to the 'clean slate principle', was more advanced than in Australia. The newly installed telephone system, for instance, was the best in the world. It ran on radio waves from transmitters on mountain peaks, but it was installed largely because of the logistical nightmare of trying to raise telegraph poles on clan land. Of course there had been a revolution in the Highlands since first contact, but as yet it was unclear who, if anyone, was the victor.

We had talked late into the evening and Akunai was tired from translating. The sounds of the village had been silenced by sleep. With a polite goodnight and a gentle handshake Baito left the hut, and Akunai built up the fire against the chill of the night.

Akunai was right about the coffee flush. Over the next couple of weeks, as the berries ripened, an atmosphere as electric and exhilarating as a closely fought football match tightened its hold on Eastern Highlands Province. I saw the smoking wreckage of several trucks and PMVs (officially 'Public Motor Vehicles', but more accurately described by anyone chancing a collision with them as 'People Moving at Velocity') – all due to an overindulgence of alcohol and high spirits. A local group of *rascals* – a pidgin euphemism for a roving band of hoodlums – had taken to the roads wearing Mickey Mouse masks and were holding up trucks with *banaras* and *spias*. At a pig feast in a local village I saw one woman stab her husband's younger wife in the neck in a fit of jealous rage.

Two frantic weeks had given me my first glimpse of the Highlands but I had barely, it seemed, scratched the surface. The pace of change was breathtaking. Already there were rumours of big gold discoveries further west near the border of Irian Jaya, in parts of the country not yet exposed to the outside world. If I wanted to confront the floodwaters of change, Akunai advised, this would be the place to go.

Akunai had never been further west than Mt Hagen, one province away, and seemed pleased by my proposal that we should go to the Western Highlands together. In a few years, he said, he would be more settled and able to devote some time to travel.

That year, I left him on the Goroka airstrip with my warmest sweaters and a dream to go *wokabaut* in some more remote, less 'civilised' corner of his country, before technology got there first.

Chapter 3

Kam Bek Long PNG

Papua New Guinea Goes to War on a Crime Wave

Convicted criminals in Papua New Guinea are to be permanently scarred with a tattoo on their foreheads, an additional punishment that has outraged churches and human rights groups. And Papua New Guineans are to get identity cards and lose their right to move freely around the country.

On Wednesday, the main towns will be put under a night-time curfew for up to six months and police will be allowed to use firearms . . .

Soldiers will join the police to protect the citizenry. A national guard of conscripts aged 13 to 19 is to be formed. And about a thousand Gurkhas no longer needed in Hong Kong's garrisons are to be recruited to train the new force.

. . . Conflict and violence in Papua New Guinea seem endemic. Thirty years ago, before the big international mining companies arrived and the cash economy reached the mountains, there were only bows and arrows. Today there are guns and a free-for-all. Gangs of displaced youths, known in pidgin as 'rascals', roam the highlands, the coast and the towns taking what they can, as a generation ago their fathers may have raided a neighbouring village, raped its women and departed laden with booty . . .

Nationhood and the rule of law are concepts little understood . . .

Michael Fathers, the *Independent on Sunday*, 17 March 1991

It was 1991, over four years, before I had a chance to return to Papua New Guinea. The outside world in the meantime had been rocked by the events of Tiananmen Square, the demolition of the Berlin Wall, the disintegration of the Soviet Union, world stock-market crashes and the Gulf War. Britain was feeling the worst of an economic recession. It was a great relief to be getting away.

There had been little in the foreign news columns, as Papua New Guinea is well off the map of European interest. Occasionally family and friends in Australia would send me cuttings from their press about armed hold-ups in Port Moresby, the lifting and reintroduction of curfew in the coastal cities, and clashes between the army and the independence movement on the island of Bougainville, near the Solomons. But precious little ever emerged about the Highlands. It was as if a blanket of cloud obscured the region from world view.

I heard only occasionally from Akunai. We corresponded perhaps once a year. One letter sent in December 1988 described some of the things that had happened to him. Its tone was cheerful and friendly, but he had seen difficult times.

When I visited Akunai in 1986, he had been campaigning hard for local elections, advocating an Isten Hailans Independens Group – an affiliation of regional parties. His efforts had been extremely successful, gaining the group twelve of the twenty-nine seats in the Assembly and electing the new Eastern Highlands Provincial Premier. Akunai had narrowly missed being elected into the National Parliament, coming third out of eighteen candidates after a very short campaign. However, six years without a break in the Highlands had taken their toll, and the uninterrupted stress of combining village life with national politics had become too much to bear.

There were not many in the Highlands who could share his burden: few Highlanders had a university education, and few had travelled. He missed the conversation and camaraderie of educated friends, the sophistication of another life. In December 1987, close to collapse, he left his wife and daughter in the care of his family and fled for four months to recuperate in Australia.

He returned to the Highlands to find chaos at the local coffee co-operative – a venture he had set up almost single-handedly the year before. In his absence, the shop had fallen into disarray, members of the management had come to blows, funds had been stolen and goods had gone unaccountably missing. The banks were threatening to repossess. Old opponents in local government were blocking his attempts to raise loans to build a coffee-processing plant. Once again, he was seeing his plans come to nothing while foreign businesses continued to cream off the profits from coffee in his country.

In the meantime, Akunai had secured a job as adviser to the Provincial Government, but the long hours and endless rounds of planning, compiling reports, making – and listening to – speeches was getting him down. In January 1991, when I was able to make plans for a second trip, he sounded more than ready to put down his pen and hit the road.

"You are welcome to come any time you turn up in PNG," he wrote. "Just let us know a couple of weeks before in case I am out of Goroka, and of course I will be glad to travel around the country with you . . . "

Then, one Sunday before I was due to leave England, I spotted Michael Fathers' article in the *Independent* – an account of the law and order crisis that was rocking the country – and began to wonder about the wisdom of our trip. Over four years, Papua New Guinea had fared as badly as the rest of the world, it would seem, and heaven only knew what changes were awaiting me in the High-lands.

⎯⎯⎯

At first glance, Goroka town was simply busier than I remembered it: more trucks, more billboards, more people. There were '*Sori no gat wok*' signs in the shop windows, and no one was wearing 'ass grass' – the ex-pats' name for the tanget leaves that Highlanders wore over their buttocks. There were women crocheting *bilums* in the marketplace, under the giant acacia tree in front of the provincial-government buildings, although the string they now used was nylon and designs included electricity pylons and slogans. But the men sat around the trunk of the tree as they always had, with their arrows displayed, idly gossiping.

The Bird of Paradise Hotel in the centre of town had been transformed from a tacky motel to a kind of up-market airport lounge, with glossy floors, deep sofas, cable TV and a fitness centre – the mark of an upsurge in foreign business. But there was a guard, a *wasman*, at the door and coils of barbed wire up the fire escape. Goroka, like Moresby, had been under curfew and, although there were street lights and rubbish bins, flowerbeds and white lines down the road, an uneasiness had usurped the old happy-go-lucky spirit of the place.

Akunai looked different too. He had dispensed with the traditional Highland beard, the bushy village look, and his face had a fresher, more striking expression. His clothes were more man-about-town. The familiar faded T-shirt and jeans had been replaced by a crisp checked shirt and smart pair of chinos. The old porkpie hat that had become his trademark had eventually fallen to pieces and he now wore a tartan cap that would have looked the part if he'd been teeing off at Gleneagles. He was clearly not as comfortable in the new hat and would remove it from time to time and remind himself of his baldness – a gesture that self-consciousness would have prevented five years before. It was wonderful to see him again. I had overwhelmed him at the airport with a kiss on the cheek before remembering the impropriety of public displays of affection in the Highlands.

We were catching up on gossip over lunch – a smorgasbord affair of cold macaroni, tinned asparagus, tuna, potato salad, pickled onions . . . every last titbit an import from Australia, while we were sitting in one of the most fertile agricultural regions in the world. Goroka's new prosperity certainly wasn't emerging from grass roots.

"So I moved to town," Akunai was saying. "Life in the village was getting me down. I'd had enough of the hard life," he laughed; "I couldn't resist the thought of soft mattresses and sealed roads."

Clearly, it was more than a taste for the good life that had moved Akunai to a prefab in a razor-wire compound in Goroka. Apart from the stress of village life and the prospects of a new job in town, another demon had come to haunt him: his age. Looking at him, a picture of youth and vitality at about thirty-nine, this seemed a ludicrous concern. Yet, as Akunai insisted, by traditional standards he was already an old man. His father, Sabumei, had died at a ripe old age in his early fifties, but the life expectancy of Highlanders, according to national statistics, was still forty-five.

"It was time to change track," he concluded. "We're good at that. It's one of our national characteristics."

He had thrown himself into a fitness programme and surprised his neighbours, and himself, by jogging around the town each morning. He had also given up beer, but that was as much a diplomatic decision as anything else.

"It gets you into a lot of trouble, *bia*. If your *wantoks* know you've got some, they'll all be round to drink it. That's when the problems start. Now they think I'm boring but at least they don't get me into trouble."

Since his move to Goroka, Akunai had been besieged by *wantoks* claiming food and beds – the inevitable price a Highlander pays for a move up in the world. The concept of wealth in PNG is very different to the western idea of 'loadsamoney'. Highlanders with status are characterised not by the wealth they have accumulated, but by the amount they have given away; they are remembered not for the pigs and shells and paper kina stored away in their houses, but by what has been distributed among their *wantoks* by way of bride prices, *payback*, loans and feasts.

In the old days, the system served remarkably well. It preserved the stability and material equality of the clan while providing an opportunity for achievers to shine. But in the modern world it's a significant handicap to those in business. No sooner has a person 'made it', than there are *wantoks* by the dozen banging on the door demanding their share. In order to preserve their cultural integrity such upstarts must, periodically, be cut down to size. PNG is hostile ground for budding entrepreneurs, and the 'tall poppy syndrome' has dogged the progress of villagers participating in the western economy since they were encouraged to plant their first crop.

Akunai was keen to get away from the present besiegement of his home, and also keen to leave his desk. But I was still concerned about the *lawnorder* problems I had read about in the press. Akunai dismissed them with characteristic vagueness.

"I don't think we've got anything to worry about. You read

these stories, specially in the Australian papers, and they're always exaggerated. Things have been quiet up here recently. But we will take a bodyguard – a *wasman* – with us, just in case there's trouble further along the road."

So, while I ordered my first cup of organic village coffee – Akunai didn't touch the stuff – we spread out the maps I had acquired on my way through Port Moresby to plan our trip into the interior.

The National Mapping Bureau attached to the Department of Lands and Environment in Port Moresby is not typical of most offices in PNG. It is a neat wooden bungalow with well-tended flowerbeds in a grove of acacias. There are large-scale maps of PNG pinned to the walls, and behind a counter, with more maps under glass, three assistants preside with uncharacteristic calm and authority.

I had had to work hard to convince the staff that I was only a tourist. Unruffled, despite his curiosity, the assistant who had served me had unfurled map after map of the country, patchworking them together and pointing out the latest developments. The rippled ranges of the Central Highlands rose like a prehistoric fossil in lurid yellow. Dotted all over them were tiny white circles: the brazen runways that keep even the most inaccessible parts of the island in contact with the outside world. There were four hundred of these licensed airstrips, some only three hundred yards long – the length of three rugby pitches – where only a Twin Otter with reverse thrust could hazard the stopping distance.

The famous Hailans Haiwe, running up to Goroka from Lae on the coast, had recently been sealed beyond Mt Hagen, branching off to Wabag in Enga Province to the north-west, and Mendi in Southern Highlands Province to the south-east. Unpredictable dirt roads, excavated since my last visit, wiggled towards the Tari Basin, home of the Huli Wigmen. Beyond Tari, villagers had to look to the sky for outside contact. They might never have seen a car or a truck, but as schoolchildren they would have learnt to recognise a de Havilland Dash 8 or a Bandeirante as a speck on the horizon or by the sound of its engine alone.

There were still amorphous white spaces, marked 'Relief Data Incomplete', on some of the maps, and here and there among the contour lines were vague, almost apologetic headings: 'Generally Forest Covered', 'Numerous Sinkholes & Limestone Pinnacles', 'Clearings'. Then there were bolder, but no more elucidating, statements in purple capitals: 'MEF [Maximum Elevation in Feet] BELIEVED NOT TO EXCEED 12,300 FT', or simply 'MEF INDETERMINABLE'. These were cartography's last scraps of *terra incognita*.

In contrast to the sheaves of charts available for PNG, the map office had only one small-scale representation of the Indonesian half of the island. Looking for a map of Irian Jaya in PNG was like trying to see the dark side of the moon, and piecing the two halves together seemed just as incongruous. But the assistant was not intimidated by history.

"The whole island of New Guinea is like the profile of a bird of paradise, perching in a tree," he had said. "Not many people think of it like that because they never look at the two sides together." But there, he showed me, was the bird's head – the so-called Vogelkop Peninsula in Irian Jaya – looking west towards Borneo, and the long tail feathers of the Port Moresby peninsula on the PNG side trailing down to the coast of Queensland. Its feet dabbled in Torres Strait. And across the divide, which I later remedied with Sellotape, furled a complete set of wings – the central mountain range of New Guinea.

⸺

Akunai and I decided to make two trips, each jaunt lasting a week or so (the most Akunai could take off from work at one time). The first trip would be to remote Enga Province in the country's 'wild west' – an area which had begun to be opened up only in the last twenty years, and where the largest gold mine outside South Africa was about to kick into operation; we would then go on to legendary Lake Kutubu in neighbouring Southern Highlands Province, where the Foi and Fasu people lived, and where a Chevron/BP conglomerate had just struck oil.

The oil and gold discoveries were already sending shock waves through the Highlands, and myths of Klondike proportions fuelled night-time storytelling: people in Goroka talked of rednecks, or *bus kanakas*, who had become kina millionaires overnight; of businessmen from Australia and the States flown in to remote villages to pay fortunes in compensation; of armed resistance and sabotage. So far neither Porgera, the mining town, nor the new road to it were on the map. And Kutubu was still a vast blue oasis in the middle of nowhere. This would be the last chance to see these regions before technology gobbled them up, and a good excuse to investigate the extravagant rumours.

The second trip, more daunting for Akunai who had never before considered it, was to the Highlands of Irian Jaya. Indonesia had recently relaxed border restrictions in an effort to woo foreign trade and dilute criticism of its tyrannical treatment of indigenous peoples. Irian Jaya's policy towards the native New Guinea Highlanders in its domain had bordered at one point on genocide, and though its recent record was more humanitarian,

there was still a guerrilla resistance movement vying for seces-
sion. Few, if any, PNG nationals had ever visited the Highlands
of Irian Jaya on a tourist visa, and this could be Akunai's only
chance to see how the other half lived. Appropriately, we
thought, a million-dollar campaign was advertising 1991 as
'Visit Indonesia Year'.

CHAPTER 4

Hailans Haiwe

At first, the forecourt of the huge BP petrol station in Goroka seemed like any other: packed with Mazda cars and pick-ups queuing for petrol beneath the distinctive yellow and green awning. But the 'No Smoking' sign was in pidgin – '*Noken Simok*' – and the skin of a green parrot swung from a rear-view mirror: the PNG equivalent of fluffy dice or worry beads.

Akunai had borrowed a government truck for the journey but it was hardly an advertisement for its department. The wing mirrors had been nicked, and the tyres were as smooth as a baby's bottom; they would never survive the notorious highway in Simbu Province, let alone the uncharted roads of our destination in Enga. There was hot air shooting up from the engine through a hole in the rubber around the gear stick – rats had chewed through it. There was no question of the driver wearing shorts: to change gear you had to sit hard up against the door and snatch your leg back before a searing blast of air took off some skin.

A small and wizened man in Aussie work boots, several sizes too large, slopped up to the truck from the repairs shop. He was dragging on a fat newspaper cigarette, stuffed with *tabak brus* –

the rough native tobacco that tears a strip off the oesophagus with one gasp. He circled the car appraisingly.

"*Strongpela foa wil draiv, disil pawa – em nau!*" he rasped, impressed. Akunai looked suitably gratified.

The mechanic checked the oil and peered into the engine, a look of concern on his face and the cigarette teetering on his lips. I got out of the car and stood well back. He carried on tinkering, oblivious, and within minutes had the car jacked up and the tyres pulled off, his sinewy arms working double-time with the spanner. There were tribal tattoos on his cheeks, and his earlobes were stretched into long loops, revealing daylight where the gristle used to be.

"*Nambawan taia,*" he said proudly, wheeling up a nearly new Dunlop and fixing it to the hub.

He replaced the other tyres as well, but was at a loss as to what to do with the rubber around the gear stick. It looked as if we would have to wear trousers. The spare tyre was rolled off into the workshop for inspection while the elfin mechanic slid under the car to look for further defects.

A few moments later a resounding bang issued from indoors and a ruffled assistant in dungarees rushed out towards us.

"*Sori tru,*" he gasped, "*spe taia i bagarap.*"

"He says he's very sorry," said Akunai, after a moment spent searching for the *mot juste*, "the spare tyre has . . . burst."

There was some confusion about what had happened, as the man working on the tyre was deaf and dumb and it took a while to understand what he was trying to convey to the assistant. It appeared there were no more replacements – we had taken the last four roadworthy tyres in Goroka. To his annoyance, our mechanic was losing face. He lolloped off purposefully into the workshop and returned sometime later, triumphant, with one more tyre. It was not difficult to see that this one had enjoyed a long and chequered career but, we were assured, despite its deflated appearance the air in it was 'down but not out'. It would do for emergencies.

To take a *wasman* with us was standard procedure. An eyewitness was required – someone who could tell stories to the clan on his return. But Akunai was also glad to have moral support in traditional enemy territory and I was relieved to have another man to protect us from *rascals*. Akunai was at his diplomatic best whittling down the contenders who insisted on coming along for the ride.

In the end he opted for Busybee, a quiet, good-natured young fellow with a spectacular beard and a permanently amused expression. He had never left the Goroka Valley, spoke little English and couldn't drive, but Busybee had a great repertoire of one-liners. I had a sinking feeling that we were taking him along for entertainment value rather than practical assistance.

We left his house early in the morning, before his nieces and nephews had gone to school.

"You taking our uncle to find gold and make us rich?" they asked, eyes like dinner plates.

"Will they shoot arrows at you in Enga Province?"

"Is Busybee going to ride in a *helikopta?*"

They squealed and shouted as we drove out of the yard, slinging their satchels after us and dancing up and down.

"Busybee, Busybee, Busybee!"

"*Gutbai, lukautim gut* – take care!"

"*Lukim yu* – see you, Busybee!"

It was a fresh, sunny morning like an English spring day.

There was a light carpet of mist lying over the airfield at knee height, and a couple of engineers wading through it waved as we passed. The first of the daily flights from Port Moresby was coming in to land.

⎯⎯⌐⎯⎯

I had been a little unnerved by headlines on the front page of the national *Post Courier* the day before.

School Closed as Tribal War Erupts

Wabag High School in Enga was closed indefinitely yesterday as a tribal war erupted following the slaying of a student at the weekend . . .

The piece had made the front page not on the strength of murder but because the incident involved the closure of a school. The tale could well have come from the annals of Akunai's village. The Eastern Highlands' past was evidently alive and kicking in the west of the country. The incident was graphic:

The student, Ango Kaki, a member of the San clan in Wabag, was returning to the school about four o'clock on Saturday afternoon when a member of the Kaliak clan confronted him at the Wakumare bridge and chopped him to death.

Wabag police said that the motive for the killing was payback.

The San and Kaliaks are traditional enemies. During a tribal confrontation in 1972, some members of the San clan chopped to death a member of the Kaliak clan, who was the father of the suspected killer.

Early Saturday morning, San tribesmen carried out a dawn raid on an unsuspecting Kaliak village using shot guns and other high-powered firearms and seriously wounded two Kaliak tribesmen. One of them is reported to be fighting for his life at the Wabag hospital. The attackers also set fire to several houses, killed domestic animals and destroyed food gardens . . .

A misprint in the final paragraph did little to reassure me of the integrity of local *plismastas*:

. . . Wabag police have pleaded with the Kaliak clan to surrender the suspect so that he can be death [sic] with according to the law.

Unswayed by Akunai's optimism, I had visited the Goroka police station for advice. The Australian ex-pat ex-commissioner who received me was the wrong person to talk to – he more than welcomed the chance to intimidate a newcomer.

"Jeez, if you're going to try and avoid tribal war in PNG you'll never get anywhere," he said. "You might as well have stayed at home."

He was full of self-importance and the trials of his office; a kind of bored head prefect.

"It's the same old problem. You get people leaving their villages, looking for the bright lights in the big city – which are never as pretty once you're on top of them. They can't get a job or a house or a car like they imagined. But they discover they're not accountable to anyone; no one knows who they are. So they start thieving, raping, murdering and no one knows how to stop them. And they've got guns now – that's a lot more uncomfortable than being shot with a sharpened stick."

To prove his point he pulled out a *home-gun* from behind his desk. It was the most lethal-looking weapon I had ever seen – and not just for the victim. The owner had just as much chance of blowing himself up as hitting his target. The barrel was a length of water pipe strapped with black masking tape to a wooden butt. The firing mechanism was a nail activated by rubber bands, and the ammunition was usually ball bearings. The Australian wielded it like a scientist marvelling at the ingenuity of a monkey. The police had destroyed sixty of these the week before, but *rascals* seemed to be churning them out just as fast as they could be confiscated.

"Amazing what they can put together when they want to kill something," he said. "At least when we were here, we kept a lid on the situation. We were a substitute for the authority they acknowledged in the village. Now you've got anarchy. Nationals don't know how to run a police force. There are blokes who could no more conduct the traffic than Alice in Wonderland. They can't give orders and they're certainly no good at taking them."

He told me about a trainee he had once asked to take finger-prints from a body in the morgue.

"He'd forgotten to take the print pad with him so he'd come back with the fingers instead. Can you imagine. Hacked 'em all off and brought them back to me in his pocket."

The ex-commissioner was intrigued to hear we were going to Wabag.

"Wayback, ay?" he said. "Jeez, Goroka's a sleepy hollow compared to places out there. That's not to say we don't have our share of drama. There were three murders here last weekend – two of them women killing their husbands; but compared to places like Wayback that's nothing. They put up with that kind of thing every day of the week."

"Careful as you cross Daulo Pass out of the valley," he added for good measure. "That's a good place for *rascals*. You're going so slow up the mountain, they've got plenty of time to leap on and try to get you out of your truck. In the old days they just cut through the canvas and got at you that way; now there are metal roofs, they have to use axes. Not a pleasant way to lose your no-claim bonus."

His words were ringing in my ears as we approached Daulo Pass – the monster that marked the western end of the Asaro Valley. But nothing could have looked less menacing than the 8000-foot mountain basking in the early-morning sunshine. As we ground slowly up, spiralling away from the valley floor, we passed women walking down to market, their heads bowed forward by the weight of fifty pounds or more of potatoes on their backs. One or two towed piglets by a string attached to the animals' front legs. They trotted along as nonchalantly as dogs on a lead; these were piglets on a day return, not a one-way ticket.

In a lay-by some children held up fronds of bright orange tree tomatoes tied around stakes. They leapt forward at a gesture from Akunai and exchanged their wares through the open window.

At the top of the pass we stopped to admire the view. We had long lost reception on the radio. Rod Stewart's 'Motown Song' and an educational broadcast on the history of the washing machine were the last we would hear until we got to Mt Hagen. The silence thundered.

"*Gutbai* Goroka," Busybee sang out to his valley at last, "hello Hagen, Place of Dread." He was still clutching his holdall as if intending to get out at the next stop.

There were few vehicles on the highway – far fewer than we had encountered four years before on the eastward stretch to Akunai's village. But those we did pass were equipped for Armageddon. They were mostly container lorries and oil tankers supplying Hagen, Mendi and the outposts of the 'wild west'. Iron grilles were welded Mad Max-style over the windows of the driver's cab, or *haus draiva*. One truck was carrying coils of barbed wire and steel spikes. It suddenly felt vulnerable to be in an unprotected truck heading into a war zone.

Occasionally, a PMV called Chimbu Buster or Isi Pisi or Nambawan careered towards us. The driver, cheerful occupant of the only upholstered seat, always waved; the passengers, who were into the fifth or sixth hour of their journey, gritted their teeth.

"Ah, *sheet!*" cried Busybee from the back. "*Mi lusim busnaip.*"

He'd left his machete, the trademark of a *wasman*, back in Goroka. There was no choice but to stop and buy another when we got to Mt Hagen, and brave the mayhem of the Western Highland's capital on notorious 'pay Friday'.

There were now signs for mission stations along the road. As soon as there were a dozen or more houses in one place, there was bound to be a *stesin*, be it Lutheran, Seventh Day Adventist, Baptist, Catholic or one of the weirder evangelical sects fresh from the States – New Tribes Mission or the Brotherhood of Bible Translators. Local wisdom had it that the latter organisation was just a front for the CIA – the brothers did precious little pastoral work and had stacks of money.

As soon as we hit Simbu Province, the mood in the truck changed dramatically. The borderline between the two provinces was unmarked, but both Akunai and Busybee knew the moment we crossed it. They were now, without question, in enemy territory. There were no clan allegiances this far from home. The people even looked different, according to Akunai.

"The Simbus are a big problem," he said with unexpected vehemence. "There's too many of them. They breed like flies. They've got no gold here, no oil, no coffee – only more and more people. And they come into other provinces to get jobs."

Traditionally, there were restrictions on child-bearing among Highland tribes. A woman would be expected to start another child only when her previous child was old enough to fend for itself. If a clan already had too many children, she would refrain from sexual relations altogether, or take herbal tonics to abort. If this failed, she might have to expose her child after it was born. The survival of the group depended on respecting the limitations of their land.

Since first contact, however, the Simbus had been persuaded to suspend traditional family planning. They had few resources other than their labour with which to compete in the western economy, and with the help of modern medicine and missionary encouragement, they started to have large families so that some of their children might find a living in the more prosperous valleys and towns.

There were certainly more people along the road, their clothing shabby, and all of them labouring away at some task. Where in the Eastern Highlands only the women tended the gardens, here there were men, too, bent double and digging; and in the villages, which were larger and built closer together, spectacular flower gardens reflected a stringent work ethic. There were beds of marigold and chrysanthemum in civic rows beside the church, lantana bushes round the houses and paper-white trumpets of datura clambering over roofs and fences. At the roadside, women wove garlands for the passing traffic. The verges were dotted with colonies of daisy and buddleia.

Suddenly the road deteriorated. We drove straight off the tarmac onto loose gravel and potholes.

"There's no reason to look after the road here," shouted Akunai, almost triumphant. "The Simbu government can't afford it, and there's no ex-pats or plantation owners to provide for a road."

Through a perverse logic, Simbu Province, by very dint of its lack of natural resources, received less funding from the central government than its wealthier neighbours – the idea was to reward those who were already producing for the good of the nation. Though Akunai was critical of this policy, particularly when it came to the Eastern Highlands which, despite its coffee industry, was losing out to gold-mining provinces like Western Highlands and Enga, I formed the impression that in his eyes Simbu was an exception.

An old woman filling a hole in the road with earth and stones was singled out by Busybee for verbal abuse.

"*Donki,*" he shouted, and tutted to himself at the indignity of it all.

The road was in a terrible state. The truck jolted from side to side, swerving to avoid one pothole just to land bang in the middle of another. Akunai was endlessly shifting gear, accelerating and braking until our nerves jarred with every thump of the axles. Hot air began to escape through the plug of rags stuffed around the gear stick. The noises from the engine suggested it was close to *bagarap*.

The countryside had changed too. Limestone crags replaced the gentle hills of the east and there was thick forest in the gullies. It was refreshingly wild after Goroka, but I was not sorry when the bone-shattering stretch through Simbu finally gave way to the smooth Western Highlands tarmac. Not before time, the Simbu gorges opened up and spat us out into brilliant midday sunshine and the bright, airy plains of the Wahgi Valley.

To either side, plantations of coffee or fluorescent-green tea bushes reached into the distance like a lesson in perspective. A field of white pyrethrum daisies was shivering in the breeze – a crop destined to be distilled and labelled with a skull and cross-bones as insecticide. It seemed a fitting introduction to the deceptive serenity of Western Highlands Province.

<hr />

Mt Hagen rises 12,500 feet at the western end of the valley. The mountain is named after a German administrator, or *kiap*, Kurt von Hagen, who was shot and killed by tribesmen on the coast in 1897. Before the Second World War, the town to which the man and the mountain give their name was little more than a patrol post. European coffee barons and missionaries settled the valley, just as they did in Goroka, and an airstrip was built to furnish them with supplies, mail and an emergency exit. But there was little development of the region until gold and oil exploration opened up the neighbouring provinces of Enga and Southern Highlands in the mid-1970s. New roads liberated remote populations, migrant workers were motivated by the promise of employment and lucrative secondary businesses sprang up in the wake of massive oil and gold conglomerates. In 1988, when Wabag became PNG's version of the Klondike, Hagen in turn became the nerve centre of operations – the last civilised staging post before bedlam.

In just a few years the population rocketed to forty thousand, with an unruly mob of transient workers on leave swelling the numbers further, sometimes by the thousand. Because alcohol had been banned in Enga 'to save the province from total anarchy', as one local government official put it, miners came to Hagen for their wine, women and song.

The *rascal* problem was worse here than anywhere else in the Highlands. Helicopters now flew in most payrolls because hijacks on the road had become so frequent. Despite the lifting of curfew, no one ever went out at night. Law and order rested only lightly on the streets of Hagen.

Busybee came out of the hardware store looking disappointed. Burns Philp (a chain of supermarkets that took its name from one of the first merchant ships to trade with PNG from Australia) had sold out of bushknives. It was hardly surprising. There were gangs of migrant workers hanging around the street corners looking for trouble. A policeman was trying to find out who had shot bullet holes through a Mt Hagen public notice:

Strictly forbidden in and round Mt Hagen Town
- chewing betelnuts
- spitting betelnut spittle
- littering
- interfering with flowers, flowerbeds and trees

Ignorance of these rules will result in on-the-spot fine of K20.00 or two weeks imprisonment.

Akunai removed our bags from the back of the truck and tossed them onto the back seat, locking the doors.

"Best to stick together," he said. We went to three more stores before we found a *busnaip*. Busybee tucked it under his arm still wrapped in its brown paper and string to avoid seeming provocative.

Despite Akunai and Busybee's misgivings, I took the opportunity – perhaps the last we would have – of going to the bank to withdraw some cash. Busybee fought his way into the crowd behind me with a mean, protective look on his face. Every miner in town seemed to have converged on Westpac, jostling for the counter with white pay slips in their hands. I was making headway only very slowly, when a strange little man with a cuscus fur hat and a big beard sidled up. He was swaying visibly and his breath betrayed at least a six pack of SPs.

"Where you going?" he asked.

I told him Wabag in Enga Province and the new gold mine at Porgera. I looked around desperately for my *wasman*.

"I *wok* at Porgera," he said, prodding his chest proudly with a forefinger. "I got *samting hia*." He bent down, grabbing the sleeve of a bystander for support, to pull something out of his sock.

"See," he hissed, standing up and refocusing, "this is Porgera gold." Secretively, in a cupped, cracked fist, he revealed a phial of gold nuggets little bigger than breadcrumbs. There could have been US$3000 worth of unrefined gold in his hand, but before I could wonder how he came by it, he shimmied away back into the crowd.

Busybee resurfaced. "OK?" he asked.

"Where were you?"

"*Mi lukim behain long windo.* It's OK. That man not *rascal*. He's from Goroka."

Beyond Hagen, the territory was as new to Akunai as it was to me. Familiar patterns began to change. Village huts were longer and their roofs were so low that the thatch almost reached the ground. There were almost no iron roofs now, or square houses. We were gaining altitude and out here the nights were cold. Houses were designed with double walls of pitpit and small, low doorways to keep in the heat.

"Look at that," said Akunai, giving the Engans some of the Simbu treatment. "They have to crawl into their houses like pigs." But the tone of his censoriousness had changed – from an ancient but familiar prejudice to an uneasy distrust of the unknown.

Busybee was amazed by the sight of his first *bus kanaka* in 'ass grass', and even more so by his youthful appearance. The man, walking casually along the road in a small woven lap-lap, tanget leaves and a neat black waistcoat, and shielded from the sun by a black umbrella, could not have been older than Busybee, who fell about laughing. Akunai was more diplomatic.

"Everyone from Eastern Highlands thinks people in the western provinces must be wild men," he said. "But they probably think we're really weak or something and can't stand up for ourselves. They probably think we've forgotten how to fight."

Increasingly, the men we passed were dressed this way, with a twentieth-century T-shirt worn above a traditional skirt. Most of them carried hunting *banaras* and *spias* in one hand. They stopped and stared when they saw a white woman pass in a truck – probably the first they had seen, other than a *missinari* or *voluntia*.

A group of children stood on a hillock and shot imaginary arrows, just as other children had done on the Highlands Highway four years before. But now the children around Akunai's village fired make-believe shot guns and automatic weapons; out here, they were Indians still, with no knowledge of *kaubois* and *raifels*.

There were more and more trucks and tankers on the road – though traffic would be a massive overstatement – most of them making deliveries to the mine from Mt Hagen. Talk inevitably turned to gold and daydreams. Busybee wanted to buy a huge house, big enough for all his *wantoks*, and to learn to drive and run his own PMV. Akunai wanted to give up his job in provincial government and become PNG's most successful businessman, or a dairy farmer, or a film director, or a writer, or a world-famous stills photographer, or a UN ambassador in New York. The more he thought about it, the more opportunities presented themselves and the more enthusiastic he became as he jumped from one glamorous profession to another. He was a natural all-rounder who, like many Highlanders, found it difficult to stick to a career ladder.

Suddenly, Busybee almost leapt into the front seat. "*Sheet!*" he exclaimed. We had cleared a bend and come slap up against a roadblock. It was a tense moment. We had nothing to hide, I reasoned, but Busybee and Akunai were apprehensive. We were in enemy territory and there were rough-looking men with axes and steel batons waiting for us up ahead. A queue of trucks was waiting on the bridge while several men with guns rifled through their merchandise. Busybee suggested we turn back.

But it was clear from the way the truck drivers, smouldering with irritation, leaned against their vehicles that the armed men were not *rascals*. We had reached another provincial border and the motley band of mountain guerrillas were actually Enga policemen checking for liquor.

As we drew up in line, a man with a *High Noon* swagger approached the truck and barked orders at Akunai. Like his colleagues, he wore army-issue boots and socks but no other identifiable piece of uniform. His chest swelled with self-importance as Akunai showed him our bags, and he prodded about with his baton, prolonging the effect. He would have made a good customs official at Heathrow.

He cast a perfunctory glance under the truck, mostly for the benefit of a group of colleagues looking on, kicked a tyre or two and then cornered Akunai against the back of the truck. Busybee fiddled with his brown-paper parcel but I had the comforting feeling he was looking for somewhere to hide it, not an opportunity to use it.

"I think we should give him money," said Akunai. "Do you have twenty kina?"

The miners slouched against their vehicles gave an envious sneer as we were waved on. They would be there until their tormentors got bored or they paid them as we did. Some of the miners were wearing T-shirts advertising Porgera Gold or its various parent companies: Placer Dome, CRA, Rio Tinto Zinc.

"What cheek!" cried Akunai, when we were safely out of sight. "Those monkeys were just *rascals* hired for the job. Policemen! What do these Engans know about law and order? Did you hear the way they spoke pidgin? Might as well have been a different language. Do they ever go to school out here?"

He and Busybee raged in high-speed Kamano, re-establishing team spirit after our meek performance on the bridge.

We wound further uphill towards the 9800-foot Kangel Pass, our engine spluttering in the thin mountain air, and onward over scores of bridges and rivers and round oxbow bends, through villages with intoxicating names like Wapenamanda, Yaramanda, Mukulamanda and Rakamanda. It was late after-noon when we reached the end of the highway and came to a full stop in Wabag: a tiny settlement with no street to its name and a river which cut it uncomfortably in two. There were some semblances of a proper town – a BP petrol station, a motel and even a cultural centre – but little else of size or status. Not quite what we had been expecting of the capital of Enga Province, let alone one of the wealthiest places in the world.

CHAPTER 5

Wayback

The Klondike had nothing on the events which had unfolded at
Wabag just a few years before Busybee, Akunai and I arrived in
July 1991. The great 'Black Bonanza' of 1987 put the tiny
backwater at the centre of the biggest local gold rush the world
had ever seen.

The discovery had come as a surprise to the geologists
working for CRA – the Australian subsidiary of Rio Tinto Zinc
in London. They had been running routine tests in a stream
unnamed on the map, in the middle of their prospecting licence
in the marshy reaches of Kare Puga (the name in *tok ples* means
'a marshy place of a brownish-green colour'). The deposits
seemed to have come from a 10,500-foot mountain three miles
away, which they later learned to call Mt Kare. A massive
landslide sometime in the past had carried huge amounts of
colluvial deposits down into the valley and its water system. To
their amazement, the geologists found chunks of gold nestling
in the mud at the foot of the mountain, some of them close to the
size of a child's fist.

Within weeks, CRA had established a base camp out in the

wilderness – a massive project in itself, considering the remoteness of the place, the interminable rain (up to three hundred inches in a bad year) and unfathomable mud. The chopper pad alone proved an engineering feat – the logs from which it was made had to be flown in before anything could land in the bog.

CRA soon realised it was onto something big. The company began to fly in experienced labourers – *wokbois* – from the coast and the Eastern Highlands to help with the digging, while the geologists concentrated on assessing the hardrock source of the gold prior to exploratory drilling. That Christmas, the Australian engineers and geologists flew home for six weeks' leave, jubilant at the thought of a hot, dry holiday with all the creature comforts and no concerns beyond too much roast turkey and a well-earned hangover.

When they came back to Kare in February 1988 they got the shock of their lives. The mountain and valley were swarming with people. Plastic tents had blossomed in the mud, and great pits had been excavated across the valley floor. The company *wokbois* had carried on digging through the Christmas break, grabbing the chance to make a fast buck for themselves. Within days the local villagers had heard about it, and had trekked in from miles around to find their own gold.

While the Australians were relaxing with a tinny on the beach, Mt Kare was thronging with moonlighters making themselves millions. There were nuggets as big as golf balls for the taking, resting in the mud like sweet potatoes in a *kaukau* field. There were tiny gold granules in the roots of grass tussocks, ready to be shaken into plastic bags and *bilums* like a crop of peanuts. And when the mud got too deep, hundreds of dexterous toes sifted about for more gold in the sludge.

Before long, tribal battles flared up between rival camps, and reinforcements began arriving from outside. Hulis and Engans clashed over land rights and began recruiting others in their clans for support. Traditionally, both peoples had hunted the region from valleys on completely different sides of Mt Kare, and the land was so extensive and remote that they had not previously come to blows. Now they were fighting each other and anyone else who happened to get in the way. By this time, the local authorities and the mining company were equally powerless to stop them.

Soon the Australian banks in Mt Hagen and Goroka jumped on the bandwagon and, according to the 'if you can't beat 'em, join 'em' principle, started dealing in gold. Bank clerks who had never seen gold before were accepting handfuls of it over the counter. But not all of it was kosher pickings from Mt Kare. Villagers quickly devised ways of increasing their yield – melting down gold and mixing it with lead to make it heavier, or simply filing down brass door locks. The banks lost thousands of kina before they caught on.

In all, about fifteen tons of gold were illegally taken from Mt Kare – possibly more. Estimates of the total village trawl range from a conservative nine million to a wild two hundred and fifty million kina – no one will ever know the exact amount. But the adventure made some villagers kina millionaires. One group of Engans invested their earnings in real estate in Port Moresby, buying up a famous four-million-kina business complex called Coral Sea Towers.

By 1989 the colluvial gold had begun to run dry and people drifted back to their villages. But there were still enough rogue prospectors to make it difficult for CRA to resume work at Mt Kare. In the end, the company had to negotiate a fifty-fifty deal with local landowners to recover the remainder of its gold. The story has gone down in the annals of village folklore as 'one for the locals'. It is the *kukboi* turned coffee baron with brass knobs on. Nothing has ever proved so galling for the ex-pat contingent, or so glorious for the barefoot *bus kanaka*.

The casuarina trees were darkening as the light faded and we turned out of Wabag onto a dirt track reminiscent of the hand-made road at Akunai's village. We were heading for a lodge Akunai had heard about that was run by a native Engan. After the potholes of Simbu and ten hours of hairpin bends, this difficult stretch of track was the last thing we needed. Tempers were beginning to fray. There was no energy to admire the neat little gardens or village fences or to wave back at children. We rocked up the hill with steely, silent determination.

Halfway up the mountain we passed through a grove of spiky pandanus trees, their hefty columns of fruit losing redness in the dusk. The woods began to thicken. For the first time, Busybee unsheathed his *busnaip*.

Just when we were reaching the end of our tether we arrived at the top of the ridge. This, at last, was Kamaniwan country. On either side stretched breathtaking views of the Lai and Ambum valleys, bolstered by blankets of deep montane forest. We stopped the truck at the foot of a path marked 'Kaiap Orchid Lodge' and opened the doors. Claustrophobia and irritation vanished with the rush of icy mountain air. We had climbed to a dizzy nine thousand feet. With magical clarity the repetitious drone of our engine was replaced by the evening chorus of whistlers and warblers, cuckoo-doves and honey-eaters. In the distance, tiny flickers of lightning played over the hills, the sun setting with a melodramatic flourish. We lay back on the warm metal of the bonnet and couldn't say a word.

Moments later an Engan, barefoot and wearing a handsome tweed jacket over his tanget leaves, came cautiously down the path to the truck. He spoke no pidgin, but signalled an invitation to stay at the lodge. Our acceptance put him in a quandary. He was clearly the hotel *wasman* and unaccustomed to dealing with unexpected guests. He wavered between staying with us and going for help. At last, in a consummate display of compromise, he stood firmly in front of us and sang out over his shoulder.

The lodge was totally in darkness by the time we were shown up to it. It was a strange, wooden shoe of a building, swathed in ivy and creepers like something from a fairy tale, with two storeys – a novelty in these parts. The challenge had clearly stretched the local builders to their limits.

Somewhere someone switched on a generator and bare light bulbs glowed to life. Inside, the rooms were musty and damp, and the walls were cluttered with bows and arrows, shields and ceremonial masks, all blackened with age and woodsmoke. A club made from a woman's thighbone hung from a rafter.

The *wasman* hurried back with covers for the armchairs and someone else laid the fire. In the corner a string of fairy lights advertised a bar and a tempting bar list. A sign below declared '*Sori no gat liquor*'. The list was pre-gold rush and had been granted an afterlife only as a status symbol.

Outside there was a new commotion. Someone was giving orders and people were jumping in response. A vigorous clanking of pots and swishing of water in the yard preceded the entrance of the bespectacled, jovial proprietor sporting a spectacular, bristling, black moustache – a *mausgras* Busybee obviously would have died for.

He was excited to see us.

"*Hello tripela* – hello you three. From Eastern Highlands is it?" said Peter Piaouwen. "Welcome to Kaiap Orchid Lodge. Well, well, it's a long time since we've had visitors, so you can see. Sorry everything's not ready and waiting for you. But make yourselves comfortable, we will have everything shipshape in no time. Looks like you're shivering. See it's not like Eastern Highlands here – nights are very cold. We're up in the sky so to speak. Why not settle down by the fire and relieve yourselves. And let's have a cup of tea. I'll send these fellas out to get us some food."

Kaiap Orchid Lodge opened in 1978. The project had been the inspiration of Dr Andree Millar, a white botanist and author of *Orchids of Papua and New Guinea*. The region had produced some spectacular finds of new orchid species and Dr Millar wanted to encourage botanists and tourists, national and foreign, to come to Enga to see them in their natural habitat. Largely thanks to her enthusiasm, the local government adopted an orchid – the rare *dendrobiam Engae* – as its provincial emblem.

At the back of the lodge was an orchid house with around a hundred local species lovingly tended by Peter and his gardeners. When she left, Dr Millar had entrusted Peter with the welfare of her plants and the lodge. Over the years she had taught him everything she knew about the botany and bird life of his district, but nothing she said could have prepared him for the problems of running a guesthouse in the back of beyond.

At first, there were regular visits from large botanical groups courtesy of Trans Niugini Tours and other luxury operators, but even then the odd tribal battle threw a spanner in the works. After the gold rush the locals went crazy, drinking and looting and fighting, and Kaiap Orchid Lodge closed down until the dust settled. But its reputation had never fully recovered. The odd outbreak of tribal war was enough to put most people off taking a weekend break up on the ridge. The big tour groups now came only once every couple of months and then only when they could get helicopter back-up in case of trouble.

"It's rare to see people like you," said Peter, "individual tourists. Specially someone all the way from England. Though I did have a countryman of yours come here to stay once. A *big man*. Politician. Name of Hessintime. Michael Hessintime."

"Michael Heseltine?" I almost shouted in amazement. "Here?"

"Yes. Mr Hessintime came here with his wife and beautiful daughters. He's very interested in trees. Loved to see our orchids. I heard that later he was trying to become prime minister, but at the time I thought he was one of the ordinary, easy-going tourists, you know. He appreciated everything. Even my old bone truck. He didn't worry about the state of the road. I used to take him up and down to Wabag in it. Very nice guy."

I was beginning to feel a little dispirited that we'd been pipped to the post in 'Wayback' by the Heseltines on a family holiday. But nothing could deter Peter from his eulogy.

"When I heard he was standing for prime minister, when Mrs Thatcher was thrown out of her office, I sent him a card – 'Michael Hessintime, House of Commons, England'. I said, 'When you become prime minister you know we are with you'. And he sent me a beautiful letter, saying, 'Thank you. My politics are flourishing'."

"I never knew why they chose this Major fellow," Akunai chimed in, conspiratorially. "When you listen to Heseltine on the news, on TV or radio, you get convinced of what he is saying. He's a good speaker in the Papua New Guinea style and it's nice of him to come here – shows he's a good bloke."

"That Westland business was bad business," agreed Peter.

"Politicians just trying to make something out of nothing," said Akunai. "It's always the same. Heseltine was just getting the best deal for his country."

I couldn't believe that nine thousand feet up in the mountains of New Guinea we were holding a discussion on the finer points of Tory party politics.

"Of course, it would be difficult to bring a top politician up here nowadays with all the fighting," said Peter. He chuckled. "I almost started a war here the other day – got dressed up in all my war gear, painted my face, took up my *spias* and stormed off down the road with my *wantoks*.

"Some drunken boys had tried to rape a girl from my clan. I had to do something about it. I have guests coming up here. I can't have people going around raping, doing whatever they want, when I'm supposed to be entertaining VIPs. So I went up and said, 'If you don't pay your compensation tomorrow for attempt-rape, I'm going to fight you'. The very next morning they lined up five pigs and one hundred and thirty kina – so they stopped it. I was satisfied with that."

I wondered how he had decided on that figure.

"Just general agreement," said Peter enigmatically.

"But you could have destroyed your whole set-up here," said Akunai, "if you'd become involved in this sort of fight."

"Ah yes," said Peter laughing, "but you know, my reputation is more important than my business. Same with everyone in PNG – isn't it?"

So this was the human face of a tribal warrior. I wondered vaguely if he wore his spectacles over the war paint.

"We're not angry madmen as people say in Moresby and Australia," said Peter, "like the press make out. We're just normal people fighting for our rights, sorting out our disputes.

How else would we solve our problems, like drunkenness, and women, and thieving and land boundaries? The law is in our hands. If there is a murder and the only witnesses are underage, then the courts will dismiss the case. Justice has not been done. Then it is up to the clansmen to act. These are not crazy things – there is always good reason."

"You're right," said Akunai wholeheartedly, "these are reasonable things. The modern justice system cannot cope with our village problems. That's why we have so many wars."

Akunai had never been so animated. As the evening progressed and we threw ourselves at a feast of hot *kaukau*, greens and a freshly slaughtered chicken, Akunai and Peter found they had more and more in common. Like Akunai, Peter had been swept up by missionaries and educated at a *stesin* several days' walk from his village. His people had embraced the Catholic Church, welcoming the new creed because it released them from so many overpowering superstitions.

"Before, people were very afraid because they thought the spirits wandered about the forests. They were in *dimanples* – 'limbo' you call it. And they could kill you if you did something wrong. The Catholics showed us that the spirits don't stay with us on earth. They showed us a place where we could put them, out of harm's way: up in heaven."

Akunai listened to Peter with rapt attention, even interrupting with parallels of his own. They spoke with an intimacy that dispensed with the usual formalities. Akunai was reserved amongst white people and women. But here he had found an ally, someone who knew exactly where he was coming from, who had shared the same dilemmas of trying to bridge the tribal and technological worlds without splitting himself in two.

Though I could barely remember hitting the sack, a wakeful restlessness set in before dawn. Flickers of lightning were again playing on the ridges. Blankets of mist lay somnolent in the valleys and a few small birds were warming up for the morning chorus. The air was chill and damp, the grass claggy with dew. The place was hauntingly still. The anonymous creepers of the evening before, which climbed around the fence posts and handrails lining the path from the lodge, proved to be various species of orchid.

I took the road along the ridge, tracing the undulating route that construction workers had excavated in search of timber thirty years before. This ridge had once been stripped of its trees to build new roads and buildings, but now, such was the fertility of the soil, it was dense with forest again. There were indigenous southern beeches fifty feet high and strapping young oaks, chestnuts and conifers, like some tropical parody of a British woodland.

Daylight intensified and a pair of mountain drongos with dark blue tails took flight down into the Ambum Valley. There was still enough forest here to provide a habitat for some of PNG's rare birds. Guests at the lodge had noted sightings of Princess Stephanie and Superb birds of paradise and the brown sicklebill, though numbers were dwindling.

An ardent bird-watcher from the States has written of the time he thought he had spotted the rare blue bird of paradise – one of the last remaining species on his list. He was just about to tick it off when an arrow came whistling through the trees and transfixed it. A villager came running and carried it off. Much to his annoyance, the American's compatriots refused to 'allow' the sighting because the bird was no longer alive.

Slowly the mist in the valley began to stir. Dogs began to yawn

87

and stretch, rolling over in the gravel of the road. An outsized pig put its ears forward in warning and grunted sullenly as I passed. A little further on a man emerged from his house groggy with sleep. "*Monin nau*," he said, with some surprise, and watched me carry on down the road.

I came across my fifth broken-down truck by the side of the road before realising that this was the sole evidence of gold money in the area. I began to notice trucks, jeeps and cars concealed behind fences, under trees, in ditches. Some were rusting where they had broken down or crashed; others, still in use, were parked within the village defence walls, dwarfing the houses like tankers in a fishing port.

Of the wrecks left lying by the road, none had been stripped or dismantled. Their carcasses rotted undisturbed. In Africa or India they would have been picked to the bones – engines, mirrors, tyres, hubcaps, seats, nuts and bolts would all have gained at least nine new lives. But here, the cargo cult 'there's more where that came from' mentality still prevailed. And the machinery which spare parts could be used for was not yet in use. In gold-rush Enga, the truck was still the main addition to traditional village life. If it failed you, it was often easier to replace than repair – even if, as was sometimes the case, it had simply run out of fuel.

The mist was rising fast and periodically engulfing the ridge. It eerily embraced a ring of stakes in the *kunai* grass at the side of the road. The tips of the stakes had been sharpened and stained dark red as if dipped in blood. Inside the circle was a gravel bed under a low corrugated-iron roof, and planted around it were the distinctive purple and green leaves of tanget. It was the grave of a *big man* killed in one of the recent battles along the road. The corrugated iron gleamed shiny and new in the refracted light of the mist – probably the only permanent roof this man had ever known.

Suddenly a faint thudding noise broke the silence. Somewhere above whipped the muffled sound of rotor blades. It was seven o'clock. As I turned on my heel, following the sound of the chopper back to the lodge, another appeared behind me. This one seemed lower, the wack-wack-wack of the machine unashamedly disturbing the tranquillity of the ridge. Every six to ten minutes another passed overhead, and I reached the lodge five helicopters later feeling as if I had weathered the worst of Vietnam.

Peter was laying out plates and freshly baked scones in the dining room with the panache of a head waiter in Paris. The choppers were from the gold mine at Porgera, he said. There were about seven of them on the chopper pad there, but they came from all over the Highlands, using the ridge for navigation. They would work as long as the weather permitted, seven days a week.

"They make a noise, don't they?" he laughed. "Like the end of the world."

It was a pity, he said, that none of the workers from Porgera or the helicopter pilots themselves used the lodge for R&R. Instead they flew back to the States or Australia without touching down in any other part of PNG.

"The gold money is come-and-go money," said Peter. "Sure people got rich. Almost everyone round here got a truck – that's seventy thousand kina. But most of them are *bagarap* now, as you can see. Some wise guys made investments, or bought properties in Australia. You can't have too much wealth close to home, you see, or your *wantoks* will have it all. Some of these guys on the ridge living in regular bush huts have big homesteads down in Queensland, educate their kids there. You don't believe me? Next time you're in Cairns, go to the market. There's a whole section of people from PNG – some of them from Enga.

"But that's just a small percentage. For the rest of us, left behind here, there's no money left. It's all drunken away, or thrown at useless things. But money is flying over our heads all the time. If we could get the gold workers to spend some of their money here, on board and lodging, on food, on guides and bushwalking – just little by little, it would soak down into our local economy; keep this place going, for one thing."

A precedent deeply worried him. The famous Baiyer River Sanctuary outside Mt Hagen, which had inspired the construction of Kaiap Orchid Lodge, had been closed down two years before because of tribal war and lack of interest. It had been one of the few nature reserves in the country and boasted the largest collection of birds of paradise in the world, as well as hornbills and parrots, cassowaries and tree kangaroos, and eighty-four species of butterfly. Already, local villagers had begun to hunt there again with devastating effect.

"There are too many of us in the Highlands to be able to hunt any more. The churches and hospitals brought us good health and food – *tinpis*, rice and cornbeef. We can get all we need from our gardens and from tradestores. That's our problem now. We have to learn to live like a big population. Or soon there will be no cassowaries left, no cuscus, no birds of paradise." He laughed. "We'll have to start making plastic feathers so we have something to wear when we go to war."

CHAPTER 6

Rot Long Porgera Gol Main

As we left the joys of Kaiap Lodge to face the uncertainty of the journey ahead, the mood in the truck fell as flat as our spare tyre. There were more abandoned vehicles along the road as we continued west beyond Wabag: great piles of junk rusting beneath the casuarinas. Only one village had taken advantage of the scrap metal to reinforce its traditional defence walls with a patchwork of car doors, heavy truck parts and tyres. Busybee was unusually quiet in the back, his explosive comments reduced to a contemptuous 'tut'.

A few miles down the road we began to climb again, carefully navigating the bends in anticipation of a tanker coming the other way. Eventually we reached a plateau of blue, grassy plains. Flocks of swallows wheeled high overhead, and dozens of kites were swooping down into the band of insects above the *kunai*. This was the Laiagam Valley, at 7200 feet the highest in the Highlands.

The people we passed along the road became increasingly tribal in appearance. The women were often bare-breasted; the men carried axes and had decorations of some sort in their hair

– a sprig of fern or grass, some flowers or a feather. Some wore hats made from the fur of a silky cuscus or bead necklaces of shells or bone. Many of the men had painted their faces with yellow clay or charcoal. Even the women wore face-paint, at liberty – unlike women in the east – to indulge in self-decoration. We passed some children completely smothered in leaves. Dressed for the ultimate game of hide and seek, they vanished laughing and squealing into the undergrowth like mischievous elves.

Akunai had once complained to me about the loudness of Europeans. But the Engans seemed to revel in noise, jumping up and down, shouting, and running after our truck with whoops and yells. It was Akunai and Busybee who were now singled out as objects of curiosity. An Eastern Highlander was even rarer in these parts than a white person, and ran considerably greater risk of getting an arrow in his chest. Busybee wound his window up despite the warmth of the sun.

By now the gardens had changed dramatically. In the Goroka or Hagen valleys, *kaukau*, taros and yams would be planted in round mounds only four foot across; here, there were domes of earth half the height of a man and the length of a car. They rose up, bare and majestic like gigantic egg cartons, the tiny shoots of new plants occasionally pricking through the surface. Where the crops were riper, the mounds were green and overgrown with creepers bearing the little mauve trumpets of the sweet-potato flower. Between the mounds, the earth was packed hard to repel rain, but inside – and this was the secret to their size – festered a rich organic compost of vegetable matter and manure. Up here, where frosts were frequent, the *kaukau* mounds were designed like giant incubators, fostering the plants in a cocoon of warmth and sustaining them with nutrients.

Busybee and Akunai were clearly daunted by these gargantuan gardens.

"Small is beautiful," said Akunai. "We don't build monstrosities like this in the east."

"*Ol i bikpela tumas,*" agreed Busybee, "*ol i maunten.*"

And like Jack and the Beanstalk, we were about to meet our Giant round the very next bend.

Despite the frequency of villages, over the last mile or so the road had become deserted. I had assumed that this was a mark of remoteness. The countryside around us had once again closed in and the road was climbing beneath the limestone pinnacles. It seemed likely that the villagers were out hunting in the montane forest or working in their gardens. So it was startling to find them massed in our path, a human blockade, as we turned another bend. Shrill whistles sounded as we drew up to the crowd, like a thousand traffic conductors out of control. The noise had a galvanising effect, whipping the whistle-blowers into near frenzy.

The crowd swarmed around our truck as we pulled to a halt; they were shouting, shaking their spears and beating on the sides of the vehicle, their faces fired with excitement. Some of them had red rings around their eyes and yellow spots on their cheeks. They were protesting about the existence of the new road and were using a traditional *sing-sing* to assert their power. Two tankers and another truck were marooned in front of us, their drivers locked inside their cabs for safety.

From a short distance away came the thud of *kundu* drums, slowly building in volume until a band of dancers came into sight. This was what the crowd had been waiting for, and attention thankfully switched back in their direction. Drawn on by the thought of photographs I got out of the truck and sank into the crowd, followed hesitantly by Akunai.

The dancers were fierce and warlike, blowing whistles and sweeping up in a phalanx suggestive of an armed assault. Puffs of dust rose from the road as they stamped their feet in unison, raising their knees high to get the full effect of the march, and kicking up their long sackcloth aprons before them. Their buttocks were covered with great bushes of tanget and their calves bound with bark and grass bandanas. On their foreheads and around their necks they wore the distinctive crescent-shaped discs of the kina shell. Their faces were painted black. Bushy tufts of cassowary feathers tossed about on their heads, increasing their height by an impressive foot and a half. The crowd parted reverently before them, intoxicated by the rhythm of the whistles and the drums, and then fell back as the dancers pulled rank and faced them, thirty strong, like some nightmarish platoon trooping its colour.

I was causing a stir in my corner of the crowd and as many faces were turned towards me as they were to the parade ground. But I was too preoccupied with my camera to notice an irate warrior approaching and shaking his axe. Eventually someone pushed me towards him and the man let rip with words of violent abuse.

I tried to apologise and shook my head uncomprehendingly, but he gesticulated all the more and began prodding me towards the periphery of the crowd. Two of his henchmen came up and muscled me down the side of a bank. Akunai was nowhere in sight and the truck, with Busybee sitting on top of it, was more than forty crowded yards away. I was being jostled and beginning to despair when one of the onlookers threatened, "You give him *planti mani*. Him manager *bilong sing-sing*. Him *bikpela* man. He say you pay for *snap-snap – kisim poto*."

It seemed miraculous to be offered an escape and I gave him all I had in my pockets. He snatched the twelve kina without complaint and I was left to fight my way back to the truck, bruised and tearful with shock.

Busybee seemed as relieved to see me as I was to reach him, although from his vantage point on the roof of the truck he had perfected an air of disdain and detachment. The *busnaip* lay unsheathed against his leg. Only when Akunai came battling towards us did he feel his job was over. He slid down to the ground and into the back seat. We took advantage of the first break in the crowds to speed off down the road.

As the sound of the *sing-sing* was left behind, our relief was overwhelming.

"We nearly became the next headlines for the *Post Courier*," laughed Akunai: " 'Three People Hacked to Death by Wild Tribe in Enga!'."

"Did you see that guy with the axe and all that body paint?"

"You should have seen the blokes I was stuck with over the other side," said Akunai.

The tension of the moment was diffused. On reflection, however, the incident took on a different perspective. We had been precisely what the warriors had been protesting about – outsiders using the road. And we had walked into the proceedings with the arrogance of uninvited guests. It was scarcely surprising that the local *big man* had demanded reparation, particularly from a westerner – a representative of the people responsible for the road in the first place. To my mind, as well no doubt to his, he had reasserted his authority by reminding me of my status – an unwanted foreigner in someone else's land. The feeling of being an intruder began to haunt me.

The road wound steadily upwards. There were no more

villages and we could rest assured that there would be no more *sing-sings*. Up here there was only forest, deep dark tracts of it filling the gorges and swathing the pinnacles. Busybee and Akunai had never seen forest like this: gigantic and dense, dripping with moss and epiphytes, alive with the presence of birds skimming the treetops. This was virgin territory, so high and impenetrable that it had never been cleared for gardens or firewood. It had even repelled the more recent interests of logging and settlement. The forest existed in its manifold glory as it had done for tens of thousands of years. It almost certainly contained species and subspecies as yet unknown: plants, butterflies and insects with no name; botanical mechanisms and biological dependencies never before imagined; trees larger than those on record; a whole world yet to be scientifically investigated.

The road dissected the forest like a ribbon-tailed snake. Money sang out from the scrunch of quality gravel, from the evenness of its surface, from the generous lay-bys designed for passing tankers and lorries, from the gradient and angle of its bends and from the way the road followed the contours of the mountains it traversed. This was a feat of modern engineering and superhuman endeavour. It led us on beguiled.

When we finally caught sight of Porgera, with its shanty towns and airstrip, it was from one of the road's superior lay-bys. The cliff face dropped away on our left-hand side, falling 2500 feet to the valley floor. The morning air had dried the limestone on the road. From halfway down the mountain we could see great puffs of powder agitated by dumper trucks on the move. Everything in the valley – trees, houses, vehicles – was veiled in dust like an over-exposed photograph. After miles of travelling through rainforest it seemed we had stumbled on the flip side of Shangri-la

– an oasis of tin and dust, of machinery and Nissen huts.

Akunai surrendered the driving seat to me. This is not Papua New Guinea, he seemed to be saying, this comes from your world – it's not up to me to see us through.

But the view from our lay-by was just the beginning. As we descended into the valley, past the busy construction work of the new runway designed for jet aircraft, through a checkpoint, past stalls of dusty bananas and black-market petrol, it became clear we were nowhere near the mine itself. This was the 'unofficial' face of Porgera. This was where dependants of the mine workers set up their camps, where the traders and merchants sold their wares at vastly inflated prices – fourteen kina for a chicken, noted Busybee, appalled, compared to ten kina in Wabag and six in Goroka. Villagers had built huts in clusters along the roadside. Akunai noticed from the variations in design that they belonged to different tribes. On the slopes of the mountain new *kaukau* gardens were being dug.

We drove on for another mile before we reached the mine site proper. A network of roads and prefab buildings with corporate logos identified the township of Porgera. The original airstrip, a hard runway for Hercules transport planes, took pride of place in the heart of the town, its perimeter fence isolating one half from the other. The mining compound itself, heavily fortified with guards, dogs and three sets of tall barbed-wire fences, dominated a position to the north-west of the settlement. The roads were busy with people: some walking purposefully in boiler suits and hard hats; others, bemused and in traditional dress, watching from the roadside. There was a sense of urgency about the place which, combined with an awesome display of high technology and heavy security, gave a James Bond feel to it all. The human ants scurrying about this surreal world seemed as dispensable as thousands of extras.

A crowd had gathered in the compound of a large, official-looking building, and as we approached a fight broke out and spilled onto the road around our truck. There were shouts from all sides and fists flying from a tangle of assailants. A man was stabbed in the arm and, quick as a flash, the skirmish was over, satisfied for the moment by the drawing of blood. No one waited around for the police to arrive. A landslide had obliterated the police station at Porgera and, temporarily, offenders were being locked up in empty steel cargo containers.

We had passed almost unnoticed in the fracas, but anonymity was beginning to weigh more heavily upon us than our prominence an hour or so before at the *sing-sing* on the road.

"This is no good," said Akunai. "Too many different tribes in one place. This place is trouble."

We drove around aimlessly, increasingly depressed by the acres of chicken wire. To the north of the town was a large gully, with a yellow river of sludge from the mine flowing along its bed, and a dismal settlement of bush houses and corrugated iron clinging to its sides.

"This is group from Eastern Highlands," said Akunai, registering familiar faces. But he didn't want to stop.

We headed on up through the town towards the mine site, although without permits or identity cards there was no strategy in this. There were 'Danger', 'No Authorised Personnel Beyond This Point' and 'Keep Out' signs posted on the fence; and women walking past went barefoot in the dust with *bilums* on their backs. Two dusty pigs wandered on the wrong side of the fence.

A tanker appeared from nowhere and dust obliterated our vision. As the chalk settled, we found ourselves opposite a padlocked entrance presided over by sentries in a patrol box. Just then a couple of company jeeps drove up, and in a flash of impatience I put my foot on the accelerator and tacked onto their convoy. Akunai had been right: this *was* more my world than his, and I was more prepared to take risks. If we were challenged he wouldn't have felt able to bluff his way out, or even pull rank. I, on the other hand, could rely on some affinity with management, even though I had no place here, simply because we were all white in a black country. It was an advantage that Akunai, despite his missionary upbringing, his European friends and his Australian education, did not have. We passed through the gates without question, and I even managed a gracious wave of thanks to the sentry as he closed the gates behind us.

There was a groan of consternation from Akunai as we carved our way between hangars trying to lose track of our convoy. "This is crazy," he said. "We'll be locked up in one of those steel containers with the rest of those *rascals* before we know it."

In the maelstrom of machinery and tanks and reservoirs, the mountain of gold was unexpectedly difficult to find. It was impossible to know which way to turn. We took the only road which seemed to lead upwards, bend after bend, and emerged at an open quarry, graded in gigantic steps and alive with earth-movers. They were excavating limestone to neutralise the acids in the gold-refining process carried out in the works at the bottom of the hill.

Before any of us could register alarm, seventy tons of dumper truck was bearing down the road towards us. Great belches of black smoke spewed from the chimney stack and twenty feet above the ground a tiny black face swivelled, seeing only the empty ground around us. With barely seconds to spare we angled the truck up a siding out of the monster's path. Only as the great engine came thundering down beside us did the driver spot us squatting like a fly upon the bank. His machine let out an angry wail.

A group of miners sitting on top of a pile of rocks had been watching our progress and now flagged us down. One of them wanted a lift to town and agreed to take us to the gold mine on the way. Busybee received him in awkward silence and we drove off round the back of the quarry to the chorus of his cheering colleagues.

The miner took us up a service road reinforced with crash barriers and a central reservation of raised earth. It climbed of necessity like a stairway to heaven, vertically into the cloud. This was one of the highest roads in Papua New Guinea and the giant earthmovers had been fitted with airplane engines to withstand the altitude. They ran on hydraulics, so there were no gear changes to interrupt momentum; instead, the driver used a throttle.

Our truck was a toy beside the other vehicles – all of which were larger than London double-deckers – and the engine wheezed in protest. On either side of the road, virgin forest had been smashed as if an angry, reckless giant had been let loose with a sledgehammer. Makeshift tracks of fallen tree trunks lashed together with wire led off into the remaining forest. They served as roads to a security fence which sealed off over ten thousand acres of mine site.

"*Em i golmain,*" said our passenger at last, as we levelled out, spluttering, at the top. We were sitting on a tabletop where once there had existed a complete mountain peak. It had been decapitated slice by slice like an upturned loaf of bread.

At the far end of the quarry a massive hole bored deep into the heart of the adjoining mountain. Trucks emerged from and disappeared into it like hornets at a nest. There were an estimated four hundred and ninety tons of gold inside, some of it so pure it could be seen with the naked eye. To the company, it was worth investing seven hundred million kina to retrieve it. With the latest – and heaviest – mining technology in the world and drill bits ten feet wide, they were coring into the rock like cheesemakers sampling a Stilton. When this tunnel was finished it would be filled up with cement and another one drilled next to it. One day the entire mountain would be made of concrete.

It had begun to rain by the time we tackled the descent. The chalky roads turned to paste, splattering our windows and spraying the trees with whitewash. We skidded down back roads near the processing plant, past gigantic fenced-off water tanks like high-security sewage-works. A sign with a skull and crossbones warned 'Danger – this water contains cyanide'. Another near the perimeter gates morbidly advised that 'Anyone found in possession of gold will be terminated and face criminal prosecution'.

Our passenger took off his safety helmet and deposited it on the floor. Not until we were outside the compound, a safe distance from security personnel, did he ask to be set down. He ran off into a thicket of Nissen huts, hat in hand and, it was not difficult to deduce, some crumbs of gold concealed somewhere about his person.

Porgera's motel – prefab, impermanent and perched on a ridge – was a first-world oasis in the mayhem of the third. Satellite TV amused itself in a corner of the canteen. On the walls, for want of pictures or posters, hung jigsaw puzzles – a Vancouver lake, dewy red roses, horses pounding the surf. Next to a pair of steaming tea urns and stacks of white china cups, the menu read: wings of fire (spicy barbecued chicken wings), quarter pounder with fries, pizza margherita, apricot pie (straight up or à la mode).

A group of Japanese in tracksuits sat playing cards. An American was writing a letter. A number of Australians lay sprawled, immobilised by the enthusiasm of Oprah Winfrey. The proprietor was amazed to see us.

"Jeez," he said, "where've you three crawled out from? It's been a while since we've seen tourists this far up Shit Creek. Specially ones of the female variety, and I wouldn't forget that in a hurry."

There were no vacant rooms (the proprietor nodded accusingly in the direction of the Japanese), but he could put us up in an empty house round the back – one of the new chipboard boxes waiting to be occupied by the mining management and as yet unconnected to water or electricity supplies.

"But I'm sure one of the chopper pilots here would loan you a shower. Hey Chris," he shouted at one of the couch potatoes, "you'd let this lovely lady use yer shower, wouldn't yer?"

"Too right," leered Chris, just managing to swivel his head in our direction. "I'd even come and scrub yer back for yer – no extra charge."

As evening approached, men piled into the canteen like refugees into the ark. The rain fell in black sheets. A pile of muddy boots grew in the passage. The noise levels became raucous despite the lack of alcoholic encouragement. Everyone had a wisecrack to make about the presence of a sheila. No one mentioned Akunai or Busybee.

Akunai leaned confidentially over the table.

"Where do they all come from, these foreign blokes? All out here in the middle of nowhere digging for something that you can't even use in everyday life."

He sounded put out.

"What's the point of all this gold fever, all this mess and

destruction, just so people can wear earrings and bracelets, and put gold bars in banks in Switzerland?"

His face was pinched with exhaustion. The mountain of gold had been disappointing. Years ago, in the 1930s, Akunai's family had lived through the first gold rush to Mt Victor in the Eastern Highlands. Dredgers and diggers and great steel buckets had been flown in to Kainantu and the hillsides rang to the sound of engines, shouting and sludge. Gold was never found in the fairy-tale quantities the prospectors had promised, but their efforts had left an ugly string of open-cast mines on the hillsides and accusations of water and soil contamination. It was all over bar the shouting in under five years. A few hopefuls still panned the streams, but what revenue they made slipped through their fingers as surely as Kainantu mud. Little profit from the mining enterprise had trickled through to the local population.

The great Porgera project, it was true, promised mighty revenues for the government, and considerable local development – roads and schools and hospitals. But the mercurial nature of gold still troubled Akunai. How much would it actually bring the villagers in the long run, most particularly those living on Porgera's doorstep, when the mountain was cement and the *wokboi* townships were little more than junkyards?

"That's the difference with white people," whispered Akunai. "They have no fear of nature. Look what they're doing. They're taking out the inside of a mountain and slicing its top off. We're taught to respect the mountains above all things. They're bigger and older than us and they're never supposed to change. But these blokes just chop them up and throw them away as if they're nothing."

He was overcome by a sense of powerlessness – the kind of anonymity which people living in a world of conglomerates and monopolies take for granted. He picked disconsolately at his steak and then rejected it. "I think I'll turn in."

Busybee wrapped the steak in paper and kept it for later. He was sorry to leave the entertainment of the canteen. He'd been watching the table of Japanese, who were using their knives and forks like chopsticks – holding their food down as if it would jump off the plate. They were the first Japanese Busybee had seen and he tutted at them in a Simbu kind of way.

"These people don't know how to eat," he said to Akunai, "like they're straight from the bush."

He'd had trouble with his own knife and fork and a tough chunk of T-bone, and the Japanese performance cheered him no end.

A chopper was expected the following morning – provided the weather let up – to carry supplies down to the Chevron service terminal at Poroma in the Southern Highlands, and Akunai and I were hoping to cadge a lift straight down to Lake Kutubu. From there we planned to walk to an airstrip at Pimaga, fly out to Mendi and rejoin the Highlands Highway. Busybee, however, would have to stay with the truck and, as he couldn't drive, find an Engan to chauffeur him to the Southern Highlands so he could meet us in four days' time. He would have to brave a sojourn at the Mendi Pentecostal Guesthouse and Akunai was already ribbing him about saying his prayers. It was a better option than taking to the skies in a *helikopta* but Busybee was still nervous at the prospect.

Sleep was slow in coming that night despite total exhaustion. The unrelenting rain mocked any thought of departure. Our house hung eerily suspended in darkness. Outside the guard dogs barked. And in the distance, like a heartbeat, rose a thump of drums and chanting from the *wokboi* compounds.

In a shallow, fitful sleep I was hounded by dreams. We were back in the truck driving endlessly around the mine site in slashing rain. Every time we thought we'd arrived, the destination changed. What had looked familiar from a distance became strange and inhospitable at close range. We were looking for a place to stop and rest, but everywhere we went we found ourselves on someone else's land. Every site was spoken for. The land was possessed. In the shadows, warriors in face-paint and feathers beat their drums and drove us away. We carried on along shifting ground, landslides falling away where our wheels had only just passed. There was no way back; only optimism carried us on.

CHAPTER 7

Go Long Helikopta

When I awoke it was late by my recent standards – eight o'clock – and a crystal-clear morning. The air outside was exhilarating as only thin mountain air can be – the 'champagne conditions' pilots dream of. Only the puddles hinted at a tortuous night. They gleamed like fragments of broken mirror on the muddy grass.

The Japanese were wolfing down steak, eggs and hash browns in the canteen. Most of the pilots had already left; by now they would be tracking the ridge over Kamaniwan country on their way back to Hagen.

At ten past nine the lodge was rocked by the arrival of the chopper, its blades thumping slowly as it came to rest on the pad.

"Perfect day for it – you're lucky," said the pilot, homing in on the tea urns. "Maximum vis. It's be-eautiful up there. Can't tell how long it will last though. Just time for number-two breakfast, I reckon. It's Dan by the way, pleased to meet you. Nice to have passengers for a change. You don't get much small talk out of a box of explosives."

Busybee and Akunai appeared with a stack of plastic Coke bottles full of petrol. They'd been up since dawn filling up the truck for Busybee's journey to Mendi. "Careful how you go with that stuff," said Dan. "It can be like putting treacle in your engine." He downed his last cup of tea and headed off to the chopper pad.

"See you in Mendi," said Akunai, clasping Busybee by the hand. *"Lukautim yu gut.* Don't let those missionaries brainwash you. We don't want you singing hallelujahs all the way back to Goroka."

"And you be careful of all those big fish in Lake Kutubu," said Busybee in *tok ples*. "They'll gobble you up for dinner. I've only got Engans to worry about."

The rotor blades whipped into hyperaction as Dan made radio contact and we strapped ourselves in, clamping headphones over our ears. Gently we wobbled up off the ground and rose into the air, almost level with Busybee who stood to attention on the ridge beside the truck. He waved a slow, arching arm above his head. We hovered level with him for a moment and then spun off towards the mountain, breaking the link with our truck. When I looked behind us, Busybee was a tiny speck waving himself into oblivion.

The chopper rose high above the compound – the fences, dogs, barbed wire and mud vanishing with height and the prefab buildings shrinking to map size. A clearer, more detached impression was gained from above, and as we spun around the ragged sides of Gold Mountain, over the exposed limestone terraces and the tunnel openings, the project spread out as neatly and cleanly as an architect's model. The site was more obviously a production line with clear objectives: the roads from the tunnels led directly down to the processing plant; the tanks and reservoirs sat centrally on the level; the yellow river carried residues and waste into the lowland valleys. On the periphery, like cells around a nucleus, clustered the mine-workers' compounds, the shanty towns, the airstrip.

But beyond this rude intrusion stretched the vast and limitless forest – dense, green and inviolate. To the north, the hills dipped slowly away to the low-level jungles of the Sepik: home to some of the country's fiercest tribes and the birthplace of Papua New Guinea's most elaborate tribal art. To the west, the mountains peaked massive and unabated towards the Indonesian border.

"That's the frontier over there," said Dan over the headsets. "I saw it once, flew right up to it. It's just concrete towers spaced out in a line through the forest. There's nothing there. Makes you wonder what all the fuss is about."

The view from the vantage of an additional thousand feet was uplifting. The mess we had left below us became a drop in the great, green ocean; from two thousand feet it was no more than a mosquito bite on the back of a mammoth. Over three-quarters of Papua New Guinea's indigenous forest was still intact, the oldest and wildest part of it flashing now beneath the skids of our helicopter. Without roads and navigable rivers, logging in this area was totally impracticable; and with the promise of vast compensation claims from landowners and the phenomenally high cost of labour in PNG, even the Japanese found the prospect of timber extraction here unattractive. Only the exhaustion of timber supplies in Malaysia and Indonesia would bring the commercial companies to PNG in force. At the present rate of depletion, it had been estimated, that was a precious fifteen years away.

For the moment, though, the forest's powerful, living presence seemed invincible. When the mine dried up and the last golden granules had been eked from the rock, it would be moments, one imagined, before it was absorbed once again within the folds of the ancient forest. Nature, from the lofty position of our tiny helicopter, still seemed to hold sway over the bizarre machinations of people. The power lines we were following from the mine site towards the south-west were there on sufferance only, constantly at the mercy of falling rocks and trees, the torrential rain and the ravages of mould and rust and insects. At the moment they stood redundant, unconnected to the gas station over forty miles away, but one day soon they would fuel the great machine with enough electricity to power a town the size of Goroka. For now their only use was incidental, as a guideline for helicopter pilots. In bad weather, though, they became an invisible deathtrap, ensnaring anyone who ventured too close.

"I had a friend," shouted Dan, "who flew under those wires for three hours in the mist without realising it. They got him in the end, poor bastard. One of the best pilots in PNG."

"Just mark my words," he added, "someone else will get killed along these lines before the year's out."

Thankfully, the weather seemed as innocuous as it could get. The morning sun cast a benevolence over the most jagged crags and spread cool, dark shadows on the vegetation beneath. Akunai was gazing out of his window, mesmerised, taking pictures through the glass. Despite his familiarity with chopper travel he wouldn't open his air vent to get a clearer shot and was sitting with a cautious twelve inches between himself and the door.

Before us, the power lines dictated a vertical track up the ridge dividing Porgera from the high plateaux of Kare and beyond. Dan approached the ridge with a look of grim determination.

"We've got to get this old heap of metal up the hill," he said, as if we were a train that might run out of steam. Then added, superstitiously perhaps, "Don't worry old girl, you'll make it.

"People always think helicopters can hop over anything," he explained, sending flickers of alarm through my stomach. "They can't just take off on a vertical indefinitely, particularly at this altitude. I have a lot of respect for this ridge."

Our ascent was, indeed, alarmingly sluggish – like a lift that threatens to stop short of the top floor. When we cleared the summit, skimming the topmost trees, it was with a bare six feet to spare.

"Close one," said Dan.

We emerged onto a bald scape of waterlogged land. It was too high for trees – only eagles and kites patrolled the skies up here.

"Now *this* is Gold Country," said Dan as we descended with a flourish over the marshland. "There's so much gold here it's painful. Sometimes when the sun's at the right angle, you can see it glinting at you from the rivers."

He turned the chopper over a muddy yellow waterway wriggling across the valley floor.

"This river's a gold mine in itself. It's supplied by run-off from all these mountains around us. It's positively bulging with gold. That little lake at the end there is causing excitement at the moment. But I doubt it will come to much. For the time being anyway it's proving logistically impossible to excavate."

The lake was actually a sinkhole, disappearing two thousand feet into an underground shaft. The river tumbled down in a great waterfall which, over the millennia, had carved out a basin in the rock like a giant soup ladle. All the gold particles suspended in the water were being caught in this ladle, while the river itself ran on over the top and continued down towards the Sepik. Earlier in the year, geologists using the latest South African technology had sent a scoop down into the ladle and pulled up pure gold. So far, however, they had found no economical way of retrieving the rest. It was hardly surprising that earlier prospectors had returned verdicts of no interest when they panned the lowland rivers; the Highlands had retained their wealth in a geographical gold pan.

We swung round towards Mt Kare and Dan pointed to a patch of ground littered with plastic and wooden stakes. The earth had been torn and chewed and spat aside.

"That's the old Mt Kare camp site," he shouted, "and those are the holes where the villagers dug for gold with their bare hands. I used to come here myself in the rush, along with every other weathercock in the business. At one point, they said the area above Mt Kare was the most congested airspace in the world. It's a wonder, without any traffic control, not one chopper went down.

"We used to hover over the holes to see if any of the diggers wanted a ride. See, they couldn't walk out 'cos they'd get mugged by *rascals* waiting for 'em in the mountains. So they'd hold up a nugget and I'd come down for a look. If it didn't look big enough I'd shake my head and sure enough, this guy – muddier than a pig in a feeding trough some of 'em – would reach into his pockets and pull out a bigger one. Then I'd lower the chopper and he'd climb onto the skids and up into the cockpit. Got myself a piece weighing ten ounces once.

"Sounds a bit out of order doesn't it? But that's what PNG's all about. Some guys used to chopper their gold right out to Australia – tax free. There's no telling how much of Mt Kare left the country in '88. Those were crazy days.

"Now that's the old lady herself – Mt Kare," he said spinning to one side. "You can see the CRA mine site next to the original landslide. It's all fenced off now to keep out the villagers. They're pumping up water from the river below to help them wash the remaining ore out of the mountain."

The landslide was a bitter disappointment after the fantastic tales we'd been hearing. The sad little mud slide down one side of a small hill seemed an unlikely instigator of the biggest local gold rush in history. It belied the havoc it had caused.

Beyond the mountain, by the Gewa River, which had thronged with panners only three years before, were two tiny camp sites: the last of the illegal prospectors who made their living scratching for gold in the surrounding country or breaking into the mine site at night.

Our detour to Mt Kare had taken us away from the power lines, so we circled the mountain and turned into a southerly wind to catch up with them. Strung out with orange warning balls like ships' buoys, they led us nearer the Indonesian border. Every half-mile or so, even over the most difficult terrain, the line was punctuated by wooden helicopter platforms for service access. They were set ingeniously into bare rock or secured by deep foundations in the wet ground.

With a fractional drop in altitude dense forest resumed, and in the treetops giant cobwebs glistened in the sunlight. The power lines were leading us into a descent from a belt of mountains that had averaged 11,500 feet to the gas drill site amongst the limestone karst of the Karius Range which peaked at around 8200 feet. With the heat of mid-morning, cloud had risen from the valleys and now lay like a thick sponge below us. We circled dizzily, clutching the arm rests and searching for a break in the cloud. When we found it we plummeted through the shreds of condensation to a gloomier, sun-deprived world below. It took seconds to recover from the nausea of several negative G's.

"Sorry about that," said Dan, "those holes can close up fast as you find them. You've got to take your chance soon as you see it."

Then he added, with some satisfaction, "But that's what we're looking for. There's Hides."

Before us rose the forest-covered mountain of Tumbudu and, perched on its pinnacle, the new Hides gas operation, no more than a single drill hole in a meagre acre of cleared trees. From it, down a precipitous cliff, ran the pipeline pumping liquid gas to the power station four miles away on the valley floor. Just below the discovery site, a secondary well was being drilled.

"They're going to be pumping ten million cubic feet of gas a day from those things," shouted Dan. "But the plant's not finished so nothing's running yet. You can see the station down there, on the Tagari River. It covers about twenty acres, but they've also got a camp further downriver and a forward base at Kobalu, only twelve miles from Tari."

Even with gold and oil discoveries on its doorstep, the Tari Basin had remained a haven from the chaotic development in the rest of PNG. It remained geographically isolated, culturally self-confident and fiercely independent. It was inhabited by some of the most ferocious of all the Highland tribes, the Huli Wigmen, who were the last large valley population to be contacted in the explorations of the 1930s.

They were 'discovered' by Claude Champion and George Anderson on a government patrol from a police camp on the shores of Lake Kutubu in 1937. But the area was so remote that it escaped much of the subsequent exposure to which valleys in the east had been subjected. The missionaries, inevitably, infiltrated in droves, 'civilising' the inhabitants by outlawing traditional initiation rites and encouraging men and women to live together – a practice the Huli found particularly abhorrent.

Huli men were so suspicious of women that they even grew and prepared their own food in their bachelor villages; they also grew their hair in accordance with special conditions until it was ready to be cut off, trimmed and shaped into fantastically decorated wigs. So God was admitted to Tari on sufferance only, and as soon as Christian attitudes relaxed, the Huli resumed their bachelor rites and spectacular wigs with renewed conviction.

As we revolved above the Huli gardens with their modest vegetable mounds and copses of casuarina shade trees, above the neat village compounds emitting wisps of smoke through their roofs, Tari still seemed in control of its destiny. We continued through the valley and caught up with the new tarmac road, opened less than two years ago, which linked the region to the main road network of PNG. There were several roadblocks across it and no traffic had been allowed to get through to the valley for several days. There was no time to spare on this trip, but I promised myself I would visit the Tari Basin one day.

We flew along the eastern side of the valley, which was bordered by the same massive range of mountains that we had crossed to enter Tari from the north. The range here reached 11,500 feet once again, with the Doma Peaks rising spectacularly to 11,700 feet. This was the barrier which separated Tari and the Southern Highlands from Enga and which, even now, presented a terrifying obstacle to pilots. The lowest pass was the Tari Gap – one of the most notorious piloting black spots in PNG and subject to momentary eclipses of cloud. Strangely, perhaps, it had an appetite for mission planes. Pilots flying for MAF – the Mission Aviation Fellowship – had the worst crash record. They had a reputation, it must be said, for flying on a wing and a prayer. Some had stickers on their flight bags saying 'God is my co-pilot'. Others boasted of flying with a Bible for a flight manual.

All of them seemed to push themselves just that little bit further than good sense alone would allow. The Huli Wigmen had another explanation: they said it was simply Tari claiming rightful *payback* for the intrusions of the outside world.

"Dozens of pilots have met their Maker here," said Dan. "I've said a few Hail Marys here myself on some occasions."

As if on cue the Tari Gap flaunted itself through the drifting cloud ahead. Dan's casual and almost continuous banter was abruptly suspended as he applied all his concentration to the challenge ahead. Around us in the forest great waterfalls crashed noiselessly and white cockatoos and multicoloured parrots were flushed from the treetops. We broke blindly through the gap and out into the miracle of life ever after. The Erave River meandered lazily in the sunshine as if nothing had happened.

After a pit stop at the Poroma service terminal, refuelled and – thankfully – delivered of explosives, we swept onward on the last short leg of the flight. All that divided us now from Lake Kutubu was a notorious limestone barrier: the series of crazy pinnacles and crevices which the barefoot policemen on the first patrol to cross it had called 'Broken Bottle Country', so painful was it to walk on. The rock peaked in impossible turrets and spires, picked apart by the wind and dissolved by rain until only a skeleton remained, jagged as splinters of glass.

When Jack Hides and Jim O'Malley led their patrol through the Broken Bottles in 1935, the first indications of human life in the region were the occasional gardens hanging like aprons to the lower slopes. But this hardly prepared them for their first glimpse of what lay beyond.

As we looked excitedly northwards, O'Malley and myself stood spellbound gazing at a scene of wild and lonely splendour. Below us, on the opposite side of the Ryan [River], a large lake lay on a platform of the divide, while the Ryan itself was seen to emerge from a deep gorge about two miles to the northwards; and beyond the gorge, gold and green reaching as far as the eye could see, lay the rolling timbered slopes and grasslands of a huge valley system. On every slope were cultivated squares, while little columns of smoke rising in the still air revealed to us the homes of the people of this land. I had never seen anything more beautiful. Beyond all stood the heights of some mighty mountain chain that sparkled in places with the colours of the setting sun.

A year after Hides's patrol, a seaplane was sent to Lake Kutubu to establish a government post, deep in the uncharted territory of the Southern Highlands. From there the Australian administration hoped to open up all the populated valleys to the north. But the war years intervened, military strategists fell on Goroka and Lake Kutubu slipped gently back into oblivion.

We cruised over the last remaining ridge and lighted upon a vision, as one patrol officer had put it, 'of unfailing serenity'. From this end of the lake there was not a sign of western development. Even now the forest fringing the shores was intact, casting deep impressions upon the water. Little wooded islands studded the lake in its northernmost quarter, but for most of its gigantic twelve-mile length it was as smooth and luminous as satin, like some mercurial liquid spilt from the cup of the gods.

From several thousand feet there seemed no signs of habitation. But as we hovered lower there was an occasional thread of life in the water, the wake of a long canoe, and somewhere along the shoreline, a wisp of smoke. There had been little cultivation of crops or forest clearance here – the soil was poor in comparison to the loam of Tari or Wahgi – and the population, a mere five hundred in number, depended solely upon the lake and surrounding forest for provisions. These people were hunter-gatherers: too few, too weak or simply disinclined to compete for an easier life of gardening in one of the richer valleys. They were a softer target for exploitation than, say, their macho Huli neighbours.

The whip of our rotor blades became suddenly unbearable. Over the busy Tari Valley and the no-man's-land between Mt Kare and Hides, our trip had been a joyride. Here, our chopper was as much an intrusion as the Porgera helicopters had been in the silent stillness of Kamaniwan country.

But Dan was enjoying himself.

"It's amazing the Foi people have got this place all to themselves. Can't you picture windsurfers and jet skis and sailing boats down there? Wouldn't that be cool?"

He tipped the chopper on its side.

"I've got something to show you over here. A bit of old *tumbuna* magic."

And he pulled us up against a cliff rising over the water, level with a ledge which was the burial ground of generations of Foi. Skulls shivered on their poles as they felt the passing current.

"Chopper went down here once. Sank like a stone. Water's so deep here it's been irretrievable. Must have got caught in a downdraught or something under the cliff. But local landowners say it was magic – they don't like us shaking up their ancestors."

Akunai was looking terrified. "Can we get a look at the oilfields from here?" he suggested by way of distraction.

Obligingly, the chopper rose out of ancestral range towards the northern tip of the lake. The oilfields were some distance away (only four or five rigs had been erected so far), but a massive airstrip lined up our approach like a fairway on a golf course. Six or seven Hercules transport planes had been landing here each day with equipment for the Moro runway and the well sites. Millions had been spent on construction so far and another thousand million kina would see the project through to the first flow from the ground in another year's time. One hundred and twenty thousand barrels a day were projected but that was only from the deposits so far located. As far as geologists could tell, the entire Kutubu area was awash with oil, in reservoirs eight to eleven thousand feet below the surface.

A pipeline two hundred miles long was about to be constructed through dense jungle along the length of the Kikori River down to the Gulf of Papua, from where the oil would be transported to an export terminal moored off the coast to be shipped to refineries abroad. The life expectancy of the oilfield so far was seven to ten years. But the scale of it dwarfed even the gold project at Porgera; it was set to be the biggest resource development the country had ever known.

For the moment we could blot out the prospect with a dip in altitude as casually as one shrugs off an empty threat – out of sight, out of mind. The full impact of Moro and the oilfield was somewhere down the line; the rigs and donkeys and pipes and platforms were the image of the future. Lake Kutubu waited, resplendent and forgiving.

We descended over an island, gathering in detail until we could distinguish the roof struts of an ancient *longhaus* stretching the length of the village, with children running across the open ground to wave at us. A row of dugouts was moored to posts at the beach, like a fleet of gondolas. We landed on a promontory opposite the island. There were steps carved up the hill from the chopper pad, leading to another great *longhaus* of more recent construction. The blades had hardly begun to slacken before a man and a little boy came running down to greet us.

CHAPTER 8

Best Kept Secret

With Dan's deafening departure – "Duty calls. There's no rest for the wicked!" – peace descended and the slow, lyrical tempo of life resumed. Someone pushed a boat out towards the island, the gentle plop of the paddle almost inaudible from where we were standing. Somewhere behind us the regular swish-swish of a bushknife cut the grass. Insects droned and buzzed. It was a hot, sunny mid-afternoon and Akunai began to look very, very tired.

But Kisa, the lodge manager, was exhilarated.

"Welcome to PNG's best kept secret. We are very happy to see you come down in our garden. Two days ago Chevron sent us messages saying eight top-ranking oil workers would be coming to stay for rest-and-relaxation. But no one arrived and we had done all our preparations. Now you have come. This is very good news. We have plenty to eat, hot water for your showers, lovely sheets. Perhaps you will stay for several days at a time."

Kisa's little son was struggling up the steps one by one with our bags, leading with his right foot. He went at double speed to keep up.

"This is my son," said Kisa, laughing proudly. "He is six years old, but he thinks he is a *big man*. He wants to take my job."

The lodge was airy and musty and cool, and built on stilts. Colossal posts and timbers, their size attesting to the maturity of the surrounding forest, supported a structure almost forty feet high. The roof, acutely peaked and sloping down close to the floor, was thatched with pandanus leaves and the walls were made of woven sago-palm stems. By the great, gaping entrance looking onto the lake sat a cluster of cane armchairs and a coffee table. The walls were hung with faded bird-spotting posters and the 'Butterflies of New Guinea'.

There was a radio in the office at the rear, but it worked only intermittently. We'd had no luck contacting it ourselves. The only link with the outside world – and little more than a psychological one at that – was the early-morning transmission from Mendi to the government post in the village of Pimaga, a long day's walk from the other end of the lake.

"Perhaps you are tired," said Kisa, eyeing Akunai who sat deflated in his chair. "Many people come to Lake Kutubu for rest-and-relaxation. Maybe tomorrow I take you down the river, show you our beautiful birds, our sceneries, go fishing. We have wild cassowary in the bush in Southern Highlands, not so many now, but many more than you have in Enga or Western Highlands."

"We're from Eastern Highlands," Akunai corrected, like someone who might have come from Mars, "from Goroka."

"Ah," said Kisa, impressed. "*Em i longwe,*" and he drew out the 'long' in the typical pidgin way of emphasising a great distance. "I've never been that way myself. Do you have many cassowaries down there in Goroka? I don't think so. You have big roads and machineries and big houses. Too much noise and population for cassowary and such like. We have none of these things in this neck of the woods. We are a backwater."

There was the hint of an apology.

"Yes, I will show you around our place tomorrow, but tonight you must rest-and-relax."

Akunai looked relieved. We had flogged the Highlands Highway and tried to keep pace with new developments over a blistering few days. It was a welcome relief to be back to a walking pace. Akunai's paradise was still here – we had arrived in the nick of time – and it was all he could have wished for.

My room, halfway down the hill and set discreetly in the trees, faced west over open water. The smoky impression of mountains wavered in the distance. The sun had relaxed its hold on the day and long shadows fell along the shoreline. A large white-chested kingfisher flew off as I pulled up a chair on the veranda. Ulysses butterflies – giant, blue and slow – struggled out of the way. The room was bare except for a plain wooden bed, a mosquito net and a table with a candle and a damp *bokis massis*. A single window with insect wire and wooden shutters opened onto the lake. The door sported a padlock as a precaution against 'daylight robbery'.

"Some people round here don't know the difference, what property means," Kisa had warned. "They get excited about western *kago*. Better to lock things up – out of sight, out of mind."

From nearby came an insistent, liquid call – a dozen or so notes repeated over and over like a catch phrase. It was hauntingly familiar. Without warning it stopped and a large bird flapped across the path to a tree near the water. It had a striking yellow head, blue beak, bright yellow eyes and a luxuriance of ruddy feathers. It scuttled from one branch to another, and I saw that it was the same bird that sported itself on Air Niugini planes and bottles of SP: my first bird of paradise.

As dusk fell we sat on the veranda, sipping ice-cold SPs, at peace with the world. Returning swifts rose and fell against the asphalt sky and frogs began their twilight chorus, rasping inter- mittently. Far away on the other side of the lake, a flicker of lightning flashed through a break in the cloud, and soon the raindrops, thudding on foliage, drove us indoors. The generator groaned into action, lighting up the lodge, the outhouse and the double row of guest rooms down the hill.

"Chevron gave us the generator," Kisa explained, "we have an agreement. They buy us machine and other things and then twenty of our men clear the land for market gardens out the back here to grow fruit and vegetables for oil employees – pineapples, bananas, sweet potatoes, yams. They pick them up and take them to feed all the oil people."

It was the first time the oil development had been mentioned, and in the heady hours of the afternoon I had forgotten all about it. But now signs of the lodge's dependency seemed obvious. The outboard motor on the canoe, fuel, the hot-water pipes for the shower and the convenient helicopter pad all pointed to outside industry.

"It is big business," Kisa shook his head sadly. "There will be big changes round here. But what can we do?"

He got up and fetched a leaflet from his office. It was a glossy 1990 prospectus published by Oil Search Ltd. On the cover, a night scene of an oil rig glamorously lit was offset by a pan- oramic view of Lake Kutubu and the surrounding mountains.

"That's what they are building round Kutubu," he said.

There were beautiful sunset scenes interspersed with pictures of a BP forecourt and oil tankers. There were smiling photographs of villagers – a man resting a bushknife on his shoulder, a woman holding a baby – all looking as though they had won the national lottery. There was even a picture of Kisa in the lodge's canoe.

"Some people on the lake want the oil company here because it has promised to build us a road," said Kisa. "At the moment, it's very difficult for us to get to Mendi to get medicines and provisions, for our children to go to high school. We have to take a canoe to Gesege, then walk to Pimaga and fly to Mendi. It's very expensive. And if you have heavy baggages, you pay extra kilos too. But the road will bring many problems. There will be accidents, *payback,* and probably *rascals* will come in too."

"And Simbus," said Akunai, threateningly. "People like Simbus will follow the highway and look for land to build their houses. They will settle anywhere, whether it's rock or dust or what."

"And they will cut down the forest," said Kisa, echoing Akunai's voice of doom. "Yes, many of my villagers want the lake to stay quiet."

The cook padded silently in from the back kitchen, interrupting the conversation, and studiously laid the table. He brought in boiled *kaukau* and a pile of steaming freshwater crayfish. Akunai looked horror-struck. We moved to the table to eat and I could see him sizing up the opposition.

"All those legs," he said, "looks like they could walk off the plate. Perhaps there is some sort of . . . ham sandwich . . . in the back somewhere, instead?"

I was amazed that Akunai, who had once given me a graphic description of how to cook human flesh (jointed like a chicken with legs and arms steamed over hot coals in a bamboo tube), could be defeated by an innocent little yabby.

"It's a rule I made for myself," he rejoined. "Never eat anything with more than four legs – or less than two."

Kisa asked the cook to come back with something a little less intimidating for his guest and launched into the plate of crayfish himself. They tasted as sweet and tender as the best French langoustines.

"When they built the airstrip," said Kisa, continuing his previous train of thought, "there was big commotions. The whole idea was new to us. It's not on our land, they said, so there is no consultation with us. Other people, the Fisu people, let them in. They got paid big money for getting that airstrip on their land."

The cook came back with Akunai's sandwich and Kisa clapped his hand on the lad's back. "This fella here," he said, "was hero of the Foi people. Lawrence, you tell them what happened when the airstrip got made." Lawrence sat quietly down at the table, smiling mischievously.

"You mean when we went to war with the oil company?" He coughed for effect and paused. He was probably in his early twenties but looked deceptively seasoned, as if he were in this world for the sixth or seventh time around. He was clearly relishing the build-up to one of his favourite stories.

"When we go across to Moro," he began (and there was a slight but momentary confusion until it was clear he was referring to the airstrip and not to the following day), "we go at night time. The big machines are resting by the sides and no one about. When we get there, we chop down the trees with our axes and pull them across the airstrip. We dig trenches with spades so no airplanes can land and the big machines *bagarap*. Then we slip away in our canoes and come back to the island."

Lawrence cleared his throat with satisfaction. We were coming to the good bit.

"When they wake up next morningtime, the company is very, very angry; say, 'Our airstrip is ruined. We will catch the *rascals* responsible'. They send officials from Minerals and Energy Departments in a *helikopta* to our island, with policemen."

Lawrence could hardly contain his glee and Kisa was chuckling in expectation of the next turn of events.

"But when they come we beat them off, and beat up the policemen and pour water on their *helikopta* on the beach, and they run away. Then another *helikopta* come again with Minerals and Energy ministers and they say if villagers destroy the airstrip again, the villages would be burned down by police. But we say we will fight them off with *banaras* and *spias* if we have to and we start dancing around them. And one of these ministers he says, 'Do what you like to the officials, but don't touch my *helikopta*'.

"Then one big policeman he pick me up and put me in the *helikopta* and say he will put me in jail, and take me to Mendi. But I say it makes no difference to me. I want to go in the *helikopta* and see what's outside Lake Kutubu. So I say, 'I want to go to jail – you can take me to Mendi'."

Kisa was laughing uncontrollably. The pile of empty crayfish shells shook with him as he leant on the table to steady himself and take up the story.

"Then I tried to radio Mendi," he continued, "to see if they had locked him up in jail and thrown away the key. But they told me they let the stupid *rascal* go, dropped him off in Pimaga so he could walk home. You see, they were too afraid to come back to the island. They knew we would fight them again.

"Since then we never seen our local MP for the lake. He washed his hands of whole business. He'll never be re-elected. He's too weak, too frightened to fight."

Kisa looked thoughtful again, and wiped the last tears of laughter from his eyes.

"You see, problem is, there's not enough educated people round here. We don't know all the legalities to negotiate with this oil company people. Lawrence, here, is really bright boy, but he only got to grade nine at school. His family can't afford to pay for him to go to grade ten. We've got no university students or anything to represent us."

Chevron had responded to the insurrection with ingenuity. They had singled out two of the obvious ringleaders and given them jobs at the drill site. The men could not return to the island, for fear of retribution at the hands of their own people. Without them the cause soon lost direction and motivation, and the islanders began to fight amongst themselves.

Then Chevron offered to build a road. The idea was greeted with scepticism by some, but most were thrilled. At last, they thought, they were getting the *payback* deserved. When the oil company dropped a D-5 Caterpillar into the forest, even the sceptical were intrigued. It was only later that they realised the machine was not nearly powerful enough for the purpose. Only a D-10 or D-8 Caterpillar could build a road. The D-5 had been a D-coy, and it was never put into action.

"So now," said Kisa, "we got nothing. No road, no new small business development as they promised. Only big planes and *helikoptas* flying over us and oilfields on the doorstep. They say they're building it now – there was pressure from the government to satisfy us. Should be finished by next year."

It was no longer clear whether Kisa was for or against the road, and Akunai expressed his confusion.

"We want something," said Kisa patiently, "some compensation for all this disruption. Something like the Fisu people got from Chevron. We can't go away empty handed when these people just walk in on our lake. Better we have a road than nothing at all."

Akunai looked down at his empty plate. His hands rested hopelessly on the table. It was not that he did not sympathise with Kisa's dilemma; on the contrary, he was all too familiar with it, as the 'if you can't beat them, join them' principle was one he advocated himself. The demand for compensation payments, so integral to Highland thinking, had saved Papua New Guinea from wanton exploitation, he said. In many cases it had halted development, so complicated and volatile was the system of *payback*. The might of big foreign business had met a formidable match with the little village courts, and had been forced to deal with them on the level.

But the *payback* the villagers demanded was so often not the compensation they imagined. Large sums of money were usually frittered away in a matter of months; and roads changed the whole aspect of village life, profoundly and irrevocably, as well as costing an unexpected fortune to maintain. Villagers were often left feeling bitter and hard done by when they saw the foreigners raking in rich profits, and themselves left in a poorer state than before. But it was all a question of choice, and villagers were often given no alternative.

"What if," said Akunai ponderously, "the money was spent instead on subsidising the airlines to give people from Kutubu cheap flights to Mendi? And if the oil people improved the road from the lake to Pimaga so you could take a truck to the airstrip? It would only take a few hours to get there and it wouldn't be so expensive to get all your provisions. But you wouldn't have *rascals* and Simbus on your doorstep."

Kisa's face lit up. "We wouldn't need the road at all. No one would come to clear out our forest for their houses and gardens, or eat up all our fishes. That's what we should do. Go to the government and say this is what we want. Don't give us a road, but give us cheap airplanes, and save Lake Kutubu."

Fired with excitement, they sat around the table like conspirators plotting a coup.

"We could get a petition," said Akunai, "and take it to parliament in Moresby. We could make a film of the lake, with interviews of the people living here, maybe even publish a book – and show it to the outside world. That's the only way to make waves in this country – to show these big companies that the west knows what they're up to.

"And we should bring politicians here, from all over PNG and Australia, make them spend the weekend and really see how beautiful it is. If people could see this place for themselves, they'd never let an oil company or a road or anything else touch it."

And so we talked, well past nightfall, with Kisa's little boy asleep in his father's arms, and the rain pattering down on the palm-leaf roof. Lawrence pottered about from the table to the kitchen, contributing fiery suggestions of his own; most involved sabotage or battle and were instantly rejected even in Kisa's elated frame of mind.

When we finally got up from the table it was as generals who had perfected their campaign strategy. Lawrence produced some umbrellas, and Akunai and I slithered down the steps in the pouring rain. Kisa stayed behind to turn off the generator. As I lit the candle in my room, I heard Lawrence returning to his hut up by the lodge, humming to himself as he sploshed barefooted through the puddles – singing in the rain.

A few moments later the lights went out. From my balcony I

saw Kisa and his little son walking hand in hand down to the canoes to paddle back to their island. Luckily, the rain began to abate for their brief but exposed journey home.

I fell asleep to the sound of frogs and woke to the clear, familiar call of the bird of paradise. The morning was well established and the sun had already won its battle against the clouds. Only a thin layer of mist remained over the surface of the water like dry ice drifting across a dance floor.

It felt as if I had slept for weeks. The kingfishers were back, and white and orange butterflies fluttered over the handrail. A group of emerald-green lorikeets screeched overhead, circling the forest. From high on the wing a piebald torrent lark swooped successfully on a dragonfly. The drone and rasp of insects thickened as I climbed the steps to the lodge. Grasshoppers plopped onto the path and a scuffle in the undergrowth drew my attention to the disappearing tail of a snake. So broke another quiet day in the bush.

Up at the lodge, Kisa and Lawrence and the rest of the staff were playing volleyball. An old fishing net had been strung up between a tree fern and the washing line. No one was scoring and there were no boundaries to the court. The participants were screaming and shouting and collapsing with laughter as they ran from one side to the other. In the crown of the tree fern, barely eight feet from the ground and completely unperturbed, sat the Raggiana bird of paradise I had seen the day before.

Kisa abandoned the game without any significant effect and came up with a beaming smile. "*Gut monin,*" he said. "You spotted our next-door neighbour. There's been a nesting site in that tree so long as I can remember.

"She don't have *fedders* like her husband," he added, and with a swoop of his hand from the back of his trousers he indicated the long, majestic tail feathers of the male. "Only men birds have beautiful *fedders*. Like *big man* wears *fedders* to make himself beautiful – king of the forest. He wears the *fedders,* makes him think like a bird, makes him dance like a bird, so he can even fly like a bird. The bird protects him from his enemies and makes him so very beautiful to women.

"Men birds are very shy, and more clever at hiding. But we know the places where they like to dance and we hide and wait for them in the forest. They know we want their *fedders.* Some people say they are our ancestors, *ol tumbuna.* One day maybe we too will turn into birds."

The Raggiana scuffled in her nest and then, prompted by her chicks, took wing towards the woods.

Akunai was sipping his first cup of tea. He looked bright and breezy, the most relaxed I had seen him, in crisp, clean T-shirt and shorts (of which he seemed to have an infinite supply). There was no mention of the previous night's council, but I was beginning to accept the touch-and-go nature of Papua New Guinean resolutions. One evening's deliberation need not be the next day's action. Akunai had slipped back into the passenger seat and the Lake Kutubu survival plan was never mentioned again. To my relief, though, he seemed much more confident and content than he had been over the past few days.

"So, Kisa," he said, patting him gently on the back, "tell us where you're going to take us today."

"We'll go to Wasemi, my village," said Kisa. "I have *samting* big to show you. No crocodiles, I promise."

We set off in Kisa's motorised canoe. A couple of large rocks were wedged between the bows for ballast, and a plastic bag with fishing tackle and bait was stowed on top. Kisa sat on a stool at the back, one hand on the rudder, the other holding the side. He peered ahead, assuming the distinctive captain's pose that had characterised him in the oil company's prospectus.

The canoe was surprisingly light. It was made of a type of balsa, malleable and buoyant, and it streamed steadily through the water, perfectly attuned to its horizontal, aquatic life after death. It had taken four weeks to make, felling and hollowing the log with axes and finishing the work with chisels and adzes. Kisa's canoe was in its third year and its life expectancy was only five.

"Then," he said, simply, "it *bagarap*. Time to make new one."

All remnants of the mist had gone and the day was as fine, hot and clear as the one before. As we neared the island we disturbed a tribe of white egrets, their long legs dangling for slow-motion takeoff. We beached amidst the collection of canoes we had seen from the chopper – at close range no longer a uniform rank but a motley selection of lengths and widths, some newly cut, others greying with age and algae.

A steep path led through trees to the village, and we were greeted halfway by a swarm of children and dogs who had heard us arrive. We emerged with difficulty amidst a cacophony of shouts and barks into the village square. Right before us was one of the largest traditional buildings I had seen in PNG. Its great buttressed roof rose to cathedral proportions, while it stretched almost the entire length of the lower village, dwarfing the huts that were built at a respectful distance around it.

"This is big *samting* I want to show you," said Kisa with satisfaction. "Traditional man's *longhaus*. This one of the best and biggest for all hereabouts."

Like the lodge, it was built on stilts from massive timbers, its gigantic sloping roof reaching almost to the ground. Its length, Kisa informed us with justifiable pride, was almost two hundred feet. But, unlike the lodge, the *longhaus* conformed unerringly to tradition – no planks, no nails, no luxury plastic sheeting to reinforce any defects in the roof. The Wasemi *longhaus* was just as it had stood for centuries.

Not that this was the same building that Kisa knew as a child, or even as a young man. Wood, rope and thatch perish – particularly in the warm, wet Kutubu climate – so the *longhaus* had to be rebuilt, almost in its entirety, every eleven or twelve years.

"That's big job," said Kisa with a twinkle in his eye, "and big job means big *sing-sing*."

Kisa looked hesitant when it came to my turn to enter. "Traditionally, no woman can go inside men's *longhaus*," he said apologetically. On second thoughts he added, "But you are special guest, and no men in there at present. I can show you the inside but probably it is better not to take *piksa*." He laughed a little nervously. "These people here," he said, "many of them are still very suspicious of western *poto*."

The children stopped pestering for attention when they saw us climbing up to the entrance of the *longhaus* and gathered in a gaggle at the bottom of the steps. Some of them gestured to their friends to come and see the *missis* wearing men's *trausis*.

Inside, the air was cool and still and musky – a different, subtle atmosphere that belied the heat and bright light outside. Slowly, with the help of a million starry chinks of sunlight, our surroundings began to take shape. A single walkway led from the entrance to the opening at the far end of the *longhaus*. On either side were sleeping areas, separated into pairs by large fireboxes. The fireboxes, sixteen in all, hung from the floor into the space beneath the house. Each firebox was made by the two men who slept either side of it. It was packed eight inches thick with clay to make it fireproof and then strapped into position with strong vines. Above the firebox, a shelf on poles supported the partners' stash of firewood. The beds were laid with woven mats or thin sheets of soft bark.

"These beds near the door," Kisa pointed out, "belong to the *big men* of the village because visitors are passing by their bed places first."

The floor was smooth and springy, laid with lengths of split black palm – the same pliant wood that makes Papua New Guinean bows. High above us, the roof was thatched, like Kisa's lodge, with sago leaves wrapped around slats of pandanus wood. At the top of the ridge, the thatch was reinforced by a layer of tigaso leaves to give added protection from the rain. (The tigaso tree could only be found in the swamps and was traded by the lowlanders for Highland axes and feathers. It had become a prized commodity for Highlanders, who liked to use its thick, gleaming oil on their bodies for *sing-sings*.) Only the strongest and most weather-resistant trees – the yiyima and dogone – were used for the posts, which were in contact with the ground.

"Use different trees," Kisa said, with a dramatic embellishment of his hands, "and whoosh! whole *haus* fall down."

In the rafters and on the walls, blackened with smoke, hung ceremonial spears and the jawbones of generations of pigs feasted on in the *longhaus*.

"We don't use earth ovens like rest of you Highlanders," Kisa told Akunai, in the hushed tones of a church-goer. "We cook on open fire. More like lowlanders. And we have our feasts at night with singing and dancing to celebrate the capture of our pig, but not in daytime like you people in Goroka."

But Akunai was in a deep reverie. His thoughts were more on

the similarities with his own village.

"We used to have men's *longhaus* and women's *haus* many years ago. But now everyone lives together in their own family houses like people in town. In my father's day we used to live like you, before the white man and the missionaries came. But the *longhaus* was one of the first things to go."

The intensity of what he was saying made him avert his eyes from Kisa's face.

"You are lucky here. You should hang on to your culture – you mustn't be tempted to tear it down because other people are living differently to you. When the *longhaus* goes, so does much of our society: our links with the ancestors, our way of life. Then the village disintegrates, and the young people drift away because they have nothing to root them to the ground, no responsibilities."

Kisa looked a little confused. Akunai's outburst was lost on him; he knew of no threat to his *longhaus*. Wasemi was the oldest village in all Kutubu. They would carry on using the *longhaus* as they had done since the ancestors first built it. Surely nothing would change that, not even the introduction of a road, *rascals*, Simbus or the Chevron oil terminal.

"This place," said Kisa, stopping halfway down the aisle, reverting to the safety of practical description, "where the middle fireboxes are, is the line that separates Orodobo clan from So'onedobo. I am from Orodobo clan – only few people in the village are So'onedobo. The line goes straight through the village. Orodobo build their houses on one side; So'onedobo build their houses on other side."

Slowly, taking in the last of the fireboxes, we reached the other end of the *longhaus* on the So'onedobo side, emerging into blinding daylight. On the platform sat an old man, his eyes milky with age. Beside him lay a hunting dog, alert and protective, his ears long and pointed like a jackal. Kisa muttered a few low words of address and the old man held out his hand. Casually, as Kisa passed, their hands met and deftly performed a PNG handshake, their fingers clicking against each other as if they were black brothers meeting in Harlem.

"Most people," explained Kisa, "the married men and their families, are out in the gardens, way out in the forest. They stay there, doing their gardening and cutting the sago, sleeping in bush houses, and only come back to village once a week or *samting*."

He laughed. "But married men sometime come back to the *longhaus* alone when they fight with their wives.

"Unmarried boys live here, but sometime they go hunting, looking for cassowaries and wild pigs in the forest, taking hunting dogs. Not many people stay here at daytime. Oh, and some people building new canoe today, on other side of the lake."

We continued up the hill away from the *longhaus* towards the top end of the village, where Kisa had built himself, and his brother, new houses. They had been made with corrugated iron and chipboards that Kisa had brought back from Moro. The roofs sparkled amidst the wattle, forerunners of the type that had revolutionised Akunai's village twenty years before.

"The oil people – they were just throwing everything away. I said to them, 'I'll take that, build myself brand-new spanking house'."

We were wandering back to the canoes when a young boy, conspicuous for his second-hand western clothes, came rushing up to greet us. He had just beached his canoe and heard that a white woman was visiting the village. Breathless and excited, he came to a standstill, thrusting his hands into the pockets of his khaki drill trousers and resting on one leg in a pose he had somehow identified as being typically European.

"My-name-is-Jim," he said, running the phrase off as if he had been practising for weeks. Then, more carefully, "Where you from?"

"I'm from England," I said, and his eyes widened in astonishment.

"I want to know it," he said, passionately. He wanted to say more but we were nearing the limit of his English, and Kisa had already launched our canoe from the beach.

"Can you come again?" he asked, desperate to squeeze out the last phrase before we disappeared.

"I hope so," I said, and meant it, more sincerely than that simple expression would ever convey.

Jim stood back and watched us depart, waving from the shore as Kisa started the engine. He looked disappointed and I felt sorry not to have left him some souvenir of England. It was hard to imagine him a few years from now, bedding down in the *longhaus* for an evening of men's talk, or working in the forest making sago. His sights were already on the bright lights of Mendi, Moresby, even beyond, and who was to tell if the Wasemi village could withstand the onslaught of the road, an alien culture and this kind of restlessness from within.

Our canoe drew briskly away from the island, churning the water at our bows. We were approaching the far side of the lake near the source of the Soro River.

"This old sacred place, where spirits live in olden days – in pidgin we call it *ples bilong ol tumbuna* – where we put our dead," said Kisa. "Now we suppose to bury them Christian way, under the ground like sweet potatoes."

Giant spiky melaleuca plants – the stuff of science fiction –

towered by the water, their image doubled by a deep reflection. We entered the river and Kisa shut off the engine, lifting his paddle into action and manoeuvring deftly over the shadows of fallen logs. Tiny, electric-blue fish flickered beneath our bows, as the forest and its cacophony gradually closed in. We drifted with the current, twisting and turning to miss low branches.

"Before all the airplanes come," said Kisa, "and before people got outboard motors, the lake was always like this. You could hear everything from the forest. We used to *singaut* to each other across the lake, like when we go hunting and catch something we *singaut* to the island; and when we go looking for people, or just calling out to each other, saying, 'Here I am – how are you?'.

"Best time to *singaut* is early morning or evening, then your message travels very far. Like this," and suddenly, he stood up in the canoe and let out a vast cry – a long, open halloo that sent up clouds of lorikeets from the treetops and vibrations through the diaphragm. He sat down laughing and picked up his paddle.

"That was what it was always like. But now there is usually too much noise – too many other things, engines and such."

We were about to turn the canoe and head for home when Kisa paused, his face tense with concentration like an animal catching a scent.

"*Yu harim em?*" he asked. "Did you hear that?", and we listened hard, not knowing exactly what for. The forest emitted a blur of birds and frogs. "Far away – hear it now?"

And then we did hear it, a faint warbling response somewhere up in the mountains. He laughed gleefully.

"Must be someone in their bush house, way out in the gardens. He knows we're here – hear my *singaut*. Now he's saying *guday*."

"*Pokunapplesos,*" Lawrence cheerfully announced at supper for the benefit of Akunai. "Like I make for the *bois* at the oil station."

"You worked for Chevron?" I asked Kutubu's legendary saboteur in disbelief.

"Yeah," he said. "When Chevron promise to build us this road, some of us go up to the oil rig to see if they want to give us other *kago* for the village." He was far from shame-faced about this disclosure, though it was blatant profiteering to the advantage of his enemy.

"Me and some other boys," he went on, "go there and, see, we are unexpected guests, so we take some feathers and cuscus skins for them to show we are friends. And these *wokbois* from Simbu and Goroka give us cigarettes and plate of rice and meat. They say, 'Come and work here, it's good money'. So I work there for three years as lumberjack, throwing bombs inside the ground and blasting out the trees to clear the forest.

"Then I work as cook. That's how I learn this trade. But it's hard work – two weeks on day shift, two weeks on night shift, then four weeks off. Then some guy, he just come in and I teach him everything, and they give him same pay as me. I been there three years more and he gets all the same. 'That's not fair', I say. So I walk out – whooosh – nothing to it.

"But now," he added, laughing, "I got share certificate in Chevron. Now all these guys are working for me. They make me money while I do nothing and stay at home."

There could hardly have been a more luminous example of poacher turned gamekeeper had this not been Papua New Guinea – as Akunai had once said despairingly, 'the country of no convictions'. Nowhere was safe from the shifting sand. There was no dichotomy or contradiction to Lawrence. Cashing in on an oil development was at least as good as sabotaging it. He would try to do both if possible. And in this way he would be acting according to the best tribal traditions, making sure that every interest of his village was covered. Conflict and alliance followed hard upon each other when it came to dealing with trouble. One way to confound excessive ambition was to be an untrustworthy, but integral, component of your enemy's success.

"So now," said Lawrence, triumphantly, "I can make *mashpotato, bananacustard, steaknkidneypud, roastchuck* and *spottydick*. I used to be best cook in Chevron. Now best cook in Kutubu."

I congratulated him. There seemed nothing else to do. If Lawrence felt that he and his village were somehow still in control of developments at the oilfield, he was surely mistaken. The oil company admitted that villagers were making life extremely difficult for them, but Chevron was not a traditional enemy – it had power and resources at its disposal that the people of Kutubu could never contend with. And the benefits the villagers would derive from Chevron's success would barely compensate for losing the battle. But if Kisa felt intimations of concern, Lawrence was blissfully unaware of potential dangers.

"You should see in 1979 when first big *helikoptas* fly over Kutubu," he said. "We thought it was the war. We thought they were coming to kill us. Now they come every day and we know the white men are afraid of us. They think we're savage warriors. They think we will kill them."

There was silence around the table, which Lawrence took to mean appreciation. But Kisa, like an old man finding solace from the uncertainties of the present in the familiarities of the past, turned his thoughts to the old days, to the time of the ancestors. "I'd like to tell you Legend of the Lake," he announced, with the authority of a magician drawing back the curtain.

"*Long taim bifo,*" Kisa began slowly, and I was reminded of Baito, who had begun his stories in the same way. He told us about the origins of the lake: how the water was discovered inside a tree by a thirsty dog, how some maidens tracked the dog and chopped down the tree, which fell in the shape the lake is today – its branches the tributaries of the Soro River, its roots over in the marshes by the village of Gesege.

But this was only the beginning. That night we heard about giant fish, wandering spirits, walking trees and crocodiles the size of houses – a whole treasury of fairy tales, a thousand and one Papua New Guinean nights. Occasionally, Lawrence would interrupt to suggest the most minute variation, and Kisa would willingly concede, repeating the correction to make sure that Akunai and I digested the most authentic version.

"Ah! It was eight frogs, not ten frogs. That's how it was," he would say, or "Yes, that's right, not absolutely bottom of the lake, maybe halfway or something."

By the time we parted for bed, I was utterly exhausted from the effort of keeping my eyes open. One bedtime story would have done the trick; half a dozen seemed an overkill. I fell instantly asleep beneath my mosquito net, my mind whirling with visions of outsized fish and thirsty maidens.

CHAPTER 9

Wokabaut Long Bus

Kisa had roped me into a day's hunting in the forest. A couple of villagers had come to the lodge to ask to borrow his steel axe and Kisa had persuaded them to take me with them. "Maybe you catch a cassowary," he said, "bring us back our dinner."

Akunai was not so easily persuaded. "My days of bushwalking are over," he said. "I'm still enjoying the arrival of the combustion engine in PNG." He volunteered to spend some time with Wilbur Smith instead.

Outside, the hunters were waiting. They stood side by side, a little nervous at being kept for so long in the vicinity of the lodge. One carried a bow and a few arrows, the other carried Kina's axe and a bushknife. Neither spoke English. To my relief, there were no hunting dogs – I hoped this might keep our pace within the realms of my ability.

Kisa introduced them as my two guides – *tupela man bilong soim rot*. "This is Sandap, and this is Simi," he said. "They will take good care of you. I told them you come from the city, that there is very little muscle on you and they must go slow or you will fall over and get lost."

"Thank you, Kisa," I said, slightly nettled despite my gratitude, "I'll try not to hold them up too much."

We set off at a cracking pace along a path, to the left of the lodge, that led directly into the trees, my parting words ringing hollow in my ears. My guides' steps were small and rhythmic, as steady as the pistons of an engine. And their feet, which had never experienced the constraints of a shoe, were thick and splayed like the feet of trolls; they curled and gripped on fallen branches and slippery rocks with an instant reflex that mocked the rigidity of my boots. I thought briefly that I, too, might be better off barefooted, until Sandap broke step to remove an inch-long thorn from his sole.

So I continued, swaying and crashing through the undergrowth, waving my arms to compensate for every sudden loss of footing. If I tripped a little more clumsily than usual, a double report of "Oh, *sori*" would emanate from my guides. To begin with, I responded politely in meaningless English – "Don't worry, my fault. Should have looked where I was going" – but the more breathless I became and the more repetitious their apologies, the more I was inclined to say nothing. It was enough to concentrate on my progress, while they highlighted my every mistake with yet another apology. Only occasionally did the response to my clumsiness alter – when I actually dropped to my knees, or fell flat on my face. Then Sandap would come forward with a deep, astonished frown to brush me down.

"*Soreeeee,*" he would say, impressed by new levels of clumsiness, "*sori tumas.*"

We emerged briefly in a clearing on the top of the ridge above the lodge. A field of tall orchids had invaded the open space, and we brushed through them, Simi clearing an extravagant path with his *busnaip*. Almost as soon as we saw daylight, it seemed, we

143

plunged back into the humid darkness of the forest. The further we went, the thicker the undergrowth became. Razor-sharp succulents conspired to slash us as we passed, and even Simi and Sandap became momentarily caught up in the tangles of vines that blocked our way. At last the pace began to slacken.

The slower pace afforded precious time to absorb my surroundings, even if my senses were confounded by unfamiliarity. Once or twice, as I was ready to support my weight on a particular branch, Sandap would rush to my rescue and hold back my hand, silently indicating the forest of thin hairs that would have penetrated my skin. Sometimes he pointed to a *haus spaida* – the sticky skeins hanging almost invisible in midair, its occupant presiding watchfully in a corner. Armies of ants filed hectically across the decaying mulch of leaves that carpeted the floor. The occasional termite mound, crumbling with age, squatted between tree trunks like some nightmare fairy castle. Flowers and fruit in garish reds and oranges broke the monotony of green with unexpected gothic extravagance. The gentle cooing of a rainbow-coloured Papuan mountain pigeon ironically recalled the sound of an English summer.

Occasionally, Simi, slashing his way through the thickets in front, would pause and point with the tip of his bushknife to some inoffensive-looking plant; this was a sign that it was to be studiously avoided. Try as I might, my unaccustomed eye was never able to identify the same plant twice, and I felt at the mercy of the forest, as discerning as a bull in a china shop.

As we progressed, Sandap and Simi collected souvenirs from the surrounding bush – little sprigs of fern or flowers, which they stuck into their hair or behind an ear. They daubed their faces with streaks of mud like creatures returning to the wild. There was no path to speak of, and at times I wondered whether they knew where they were going, so indiscriminate seemed our direction. I had moments of unjustifiable unease when I considered my reliance on them. But every time we came to a river, it was always at a bridge, albeit of casual design: a slippery tree trunk felled across the narrowest strait, a collaboration of branches and rocks; or just a stake or two posted in the riverbank as handrails.

When it came to a slippery tree trunk over a torrential river, I would have much preferred to haul myself astride it and conquer the obstacle inch by humiliating inch on my bottom. But Sandap clearly thought this was unnecessary and insisted on leading me by the hand, the acrobat guiding the clown. His grip, however, was steady and sympathetic. He could see that wet rubber on wet moss and rain-polished wood was a handicap, not an advantage. His deliberate and resolute steps provided me with miraculous balance, and I held his gaze like a child willing herself to walk. When I looked back over the gushing torrent I had just crossed, it was with weak-kneed pride.

After several hours of walking, or slithering, Simi and Sandap began to pay much more attention to the surrounding bush. Simi would wander off course, following signs that were blatant to him but completely invisible to me. By way of explanation, Sandap would indicate a broken twig or an unusual scattering of leaves. "*Muruk*," he would say, and we would imagine the great cassowary bird, as big and fierce as an ostrich, thundering through the undergrowth, its naked red and blue head swivelling on the lookout for hunters like us. Simi would show obvious signs of excitement when he found a spoor and call Sandap and me over to have a look. The droppings of the cassowary looked like a fetid heap of vomit, yellow with bile and lumpy with half-digested berries.

145

"Tripela de," Simi would say, holding up two fingers and his thumb to indicate the age of his find, or, more enthusiastically, as if he were thumbing a lift, *"Wanpela de."*

But their discoveries did not quicken our pace. The signs would have to be fresher to indicate that we were close to our quarry. A bush laden with ripe berries was more encouraging – it suggested that we were in an area where the cassowary had not yet been, and that it was perhaps nearby, feasting on fresh fruit. Then we would advance like Mohicans, peering into the middle distance for a sighting of the distinctive horn that sits on top of the cassowary's head like some crazy crash helmet.

But we never found our bird. However exciting it would have been to see the creature in the wild, its reputation was enough to make me thankful for missing it. At five feet tall and weighing up to one hundred and thirty pounds, it was the largest land creature in the whole of New Guinea. It had vicious claws and beak, a powerful kick, and pointed quills like darts on the leading edge of its stunted and flightless wings. It had been known to tear people apart. But its flesh could also feed a generous number of people and the capture of a cassowary was almost always an excuse for a *sing-sing*.

Not long after lunch – a modest intake of bananas and smoky-grey sweet potatoes – Simi found justification for our efforts. We came across the great, rotting trunk of a sago palm, or *saksak*. It was standing valiantly like the torso of a dismembered giant, but the largest of its limbs now lay on the ground in fragments around it. Simi stripped off a thick, dusty plate of bark and watched the bugs and beetles fall to the ground. Further up the trunk he uncovered a nest of cockroaches, their shiny backs seething in frantic disarray. But this was not what he was looking for. Having taken stock of the condition of the trunk, he set to with his axe, tearing into the soft flesh and ripping it off in chunks with his hands. He stopped for a moment and looked critically at the cutting edge of his axe, running his finger down it and picking at an aggravating nick. Sandap also had a look and shook his head, muttering something disparaging in Foi.

Gingerly, I pulled out the tiny diamond steel that a friend had given me for the trip. The two hunters looked on with rapt attention as I took it out of its wallet. Straightaway, Simi surrendered the axe, propping it up against a rock so I could sharpen it. There was very little I could do except try and beat it back into shape and smooth over its edge. But Simi and Sandap were impressed and I felt myself rise a few precious notches in their estimation. At least I could contribute something other than squelching boots and heavy breathing to our trip. I was relieved, too, that they did not want me to make them a present of my steel; they accepted unconditionally that it was mine.

Simi set to work with renewed vigour and within seconds had gouged a large chunk out of the tree. Deep inside the trunk he found what he was looking for.

"*Binatang,*" explained Sandap, "*binatang bilong saksak,*" and he pointed to a large, fat, yellow maggot, its black head waving back and forth. Simi squeezed the front few segments gently between two fingers and pulled it from its hole. The body that followed was several inches long, thick and clumsy, and it flicked about helplessly as Simi held it up on show. He motioned with his free hand to his mouth and then held the maggot towards me. For a horrible moment I thought he was expecting me to eat it alive and wriggling on the spot.

But Sandap had come forward with a handful of large, soft leaves in which he was preparing to wrap it. This delicacy, I realised with relief, was to take away, not to eat here. I shook my

147

head and gestured at Simi, implying "Please, no, you have it – I insist." Simi grinned and laid the maggot on the leaves, where it rolled and flipped about helplessly like a fish out of water. Within minutes, two more maggots were found – one even larger and fatter than the first; the other a little smaller, but long and thin. Somehow, it was the variation in their shapes that made me squeamish – they took on unnerving characteristics. I had always imagined maggots to be indistinguishable from each other.

Simi searched every likely area of the tree, finding only two more maggots, before abandoning his task. We moved on, Sandap wrapping the maggots in neat green parcels like giant dolmades and placing them in his *bilum*. The sense of urgency had gone from the proceedings. We wouldn't be returning empty-handed.

Even when the third or fourth helicopter resounded above our heads, I found it difficult to reconcile the dense, humid forest through which I was struggling with the omnipresence of the outside world. The wooden room key in my pocket was a talisman from the other side of the looking glass. It was only when we came across stakes for the new road through the forest that the two worlds became one. Waterproof fluorescent markers were planted at forty-yard intervals along a cleared track as straight and resolute as a Roman road. As I walked along the track, taking full advantage of the sunlight and the easy terrain, I found it difficult to imagine how Simi and Sandap made sense of this development. We walked on in silence along the ghost of a tarmac road.

Slowly, as we approached the lake, the forest began to show signs of human life. Well-worn tracks meandered through the undergrowth and soon, as even these diminished and the trees thinned, we came across bush huts and gardens. The path broadened through a plantation of young black palms and we emerged in a village. The *longhaus* here was not as grand or impressive as at Wasemi but it was well populated with men, lying around on the steps, smoking, chatting and dozing in the oppressive silence of the afternoon as if they were in the piazza of a Mediterranean village. They had assembled in preparation for a night's spear-fishing, while the women were out for the day with their nets.

After the customary greetings, we joined the muddy byway of the Nipa-Mendi road. The heat out in the open was intense, yet it seemed to have no effect on the deep puddles of clay that clung to the ruts in the road. The walk was becoming laborious when we turned at last into the pineapple plantation behind Kutubu Lodge. As we carefully picked our way through Chevron's seedlings, each protected from the sun with a tiny hat of dried leaves, all I could think of was total and lengthy immersion in the lake, which glistened a beckoning blue below us.

Simi and Sandap veered off towards the cookhouse to return the axe. Their handshakes were firm and friendly, and they smiled when we said goodbye. I had not brought them luck on the hunt, but I had provided them with a wealth of hilarious stories with which to feed their families that night.

Akunai was sitting in the shade of the veranda, chatting with Kisa as if they had hardly moved since breakfast.

"What did you find us for dinner?" asked Kisa, as I collapsed into a chair beside him.

"A nice, juicy cuscus would do me fine," said Akunai, "or a cassowary steak, or a young roast pigeon – or perhaps even," and he raised his eyebrows in mock hopefulness, "pork chops?"

"How about a handful of sago grubs?" I said, pulling off my slimy boots and examining my feet, "oh – and a couple of leeches."

CHAPTER 10

Big Balus Long Mendi

Kisa was used to the comings and goings of travellers and took their departure in his stride. He believed that all those who wanted to come back, would. He was sure he would see us again. But the visitors' book was full of messages from people as sad to leave as we were. The most poignant were written by Papua New Guineans.

24/4/90
Its nice and this is PNG. Best Kept Secret would be better Life for future.

Likage

7 July 1990
What a lovely place to live in? Natural Environment is Paradise, hopefully Western civilisation doesn't pollute the beautiful lakes because of the oil discovery. Hope it remains untouched.

Phillip Kane Iyasou PO Box 69 Tari SHP

16 DEC, 90 Wesley Wes Wilson
If youd stay in Kutubu lodge, its one relaxing place, And also when you are in lodge you will over look the blue lake Kutubu

and also you will hear bird of paradis calleding here and their,
And it quite place

> Metenda Green Valley, Longo Village, Mendi SHP

1/1/91

Certainly Kutubu Lodge will one day become Tourist Attraction
and indeed a World Wonder for all PNG citizens to come and
Relax. Please at all Cost – Preserve it and make it free from
Rascalism and ensure it is a Little Heaven for all good abiding
Citizens.

Feel at Home – I did for the last night and preferrably for a
day or two.

> With Sweet Regards
> SAMPSON PETER ENDEHIPA

The last entry before my own was from a Foi villager.

09/06/91

Kutubu Lodge is in my own home area. Yet I can boast of my
beautiful sceneries and cool environment. Nature has been here
with me forever.

I should invite you all to stay with me and enjoy with me
with these lovely sceneries. Most welcome.

> Barry Fagena. Lake Kutubu. S.H.P.

The bird of paradise was sitting peacefully on her nest in the
volleyball court when we left. I wondered if she would still be
nesting there next year. Kisa was hatching a plan to put one of
her chicks in a cage in the lodge.

"White people like to see bird of paradise," he had said. "Next
year we keep one here in dining room for all to see – pride of
place."

Sadly, he was probably right. Some tourists might find a real
bird of paradise swinging over their dinner irresistible.

It was a dull morning, damp with the promise of rain. The far shore had completely disappeared, and even the island was a distant spectre in the mist. The trees around us loomed dark and indistinct. We were not particularly looking forward to our trip over the lake to Gesege.

"I hope Kisa knows the way in his head," said Akunai. "We'll hardly be able to see the end of the canoe in all this fog."

Kisa seemed unconcerned by the weather, and his little boy crouched at his feet on the floor of the canoe, eager for the adventure. But Akunai's anxiety was catching, and the eerie flatness of the light began to tease the imagination. We had been out half an hour in open water, with only the faintest image of the shore to guide us, when it began to pour. Hard, icy raindrops thudded inside the boat like gravel on a drum. The surface of the water erupted as if it had come under machine-gun fire. Kisa brought out an umbrella and held it over his son; Akunai and I futilely covered our heads with plastic bags, wincing as the cold water poured down our necks. Within seconds we were completely drenched. We began bailing for our lives.

"It's no problem," shouted Kisa over the deafening rain, "this won't last long. Just keep all the water out of the bottom and we'll be OK."

There was nowhere to land: the nearest shore was sheer cliff. Our tin cups rattled frantically against the insides of the canoe. Kisa's son was using a gourd to better effect, and between us we kept the water level down to a couple of inches while Kisa ploughed on at full throttle, his eyes glued to some invisible point in the distance.

As suddenly as it had begun, the deluge abated. Kisa folded his umbrella, shaking it neatly over the side, and laughed. "You two, so frightened by a little drop of rain. The lake only swallows up its enemies. We're in no trouble." But behind us, high on a platform in the cliff face, grinned the skulls we had passed in our helicopter. Akunai blanched.

Our parting at Gesege was brief and unmomentous. Kisa deposited us and our bags at the foot of the village. He was expecting another visit from the oil company and was eager to get back. I took his brevity as a sign of confidence; only Akunai and I had something to lose in saying goodbye and leaving.

"See you fellas again," Kisa said, smiling and shaking Akunai's hand. "I'll tell Lawrence to chop the legs off your yabbies next time. Maybe you can eat them with your eyes shut." And he was off, his little boy taking up the privileged position at the front of the canoe for the ride home.

After the humiliation of bushwalking with Simi and Sandap, the trek from Gesege to Pimaga was a breeze. The road was chalk and deeply rutted; it served Gesege's only vehicle – a clapped-out Massey Fergusson tractor – and for the pedestrian, it was a joy. It was broad enough to receive a *frisson* of wind and, as it snaked into the foothills, commanded breathtaking views.

After a few hours we came to richer soil, clearings, plantations, even some cattle grazing. We met our first villagers, carrying hoes and axes and piglets.

"*Appynoon,*" they chorused, reaching forward to click fingers, "*appynoon, tupela.*"

An old couple were plodding along the road wearing hairnets and towelling dressing-gowns. They stopped and gazed after us with watery eyes and rotten smiles. Everyone expected a handshake. Sometimes we were stopped for minutes at a time, as if we were royalty, and were offered sweet potato, taro and fibrous sticks of sugar cane. As we neared the patrol post, village houses once again displayed modern features – tin roofs, chimneys, windows. Pimaga was indicative of the times, clustered protectively around the airstrip, one step closer to the modern world.

The guesthouse, on the outskirts of the village, was the brainchild of an English *voluntia* – one of the dozens of young idealists who flock to Papua New Guinea for a couple of years under the auspices of organisations such as the Canadian University Services Overseas or the Britsh Voluntary Service Overseas or the Peace Corps. Elsewhere in the third world their work is remarkably productive and long-lasting. But like most of their efforts in PNG, the project at Pimaga had fallen prey to cultural resistance and neglect. The Pimaga Guesthouse was a shadow of its former self, though Douglas, the volunteer, had left only three years before. Experimental gardens and fruit trees were entangled with sedge grass and creepers; trellises and beanpoles, arches and supports, rotted where they stood. A rainwater tank no longer held water. Windows were broken. The veranda was collapsing. Inside, the bedding was damp, the woodstove blocked and the floor littered with typewritten pages. Only a recipe for 'breakfast pancakes' still clung to the notice board in the office.

It was a familiar syndrome. Most projects in the Highlands survive for the two to three years during which the volunteer presides over them. Market gardens – religiously nurtured and fertilised, protected by polythene and pesticide – flourish for a while with a kaleidoscope of new produce: strawberries and broad beans, spinach and loganberries, tomatoes and peas. Guesthouses and workshops, little bastions of intermediate technology, thrive on a diet of enthusiasm and hope. Then the volunteer's commission comes to an end and they fly back to the real world. A few loyal disciples continue the work, make reports, attend to the accounts; but gradually, the forces of decay creep in. The novelty fades as other village tasks take priority.

Precious polythene is borrowed to mend a leaking roof. A couple of chairs are split for kindling during an unexpected storm. The fertiliser is raided by pigs. A plague of caterpillars ravages a crop. Tools are broken and never replaced. The ledgers become mildewed. Soon even the die-hards accept defeat.

The conclusion many volunteers come to, as they battle against the inevitable, is that Papua New Guinea is simply not ready for aid. Its people are not about to starve, lose their homes or become dispossessed. Health care, education and the standard of living have improved in the decades since independence. And a cargo cult 'there's more where that came from' attitude still prevails from colonial times. If one white volunteer leaves disillusioned, another will take their place tomorrow, bringing more tools, more seeds, more polythene and more bright ideas.

No matter what warnings are given regarding the pressures of population growth, the benefits of staying on the land rather than drifting towards the cities, the need for sustained agricultural growth and new farming techniques or the advantages of indigenous business, Highlanders in PNG find it hard to see further than their next crop of *kaukau*. According to most aid agencies in the country, conditions will have to get a lot worse before the villagers see their way towards making improvements for themselves.

That night I was haunted by a weird, persistent wailing. In semi-sleep I imagined it was the spirits of the ancestors – *ol tambaran* – returning to claim Akunai or to hound me off their land. They seemed as powerful as trees and they howled like wolves. It was impossible to read their faces – to know whether they were angry or sad or pleading. They gestured impatiently and I grew more and more frustrated as I tried to understand.

The sound was so distressing that it finally woke me, and I found Douglas's old cat crying at the window. She purred madly when I let her in, demanding food, and then, sometime in the night, she slipped in between the blankets. Despite a niggling anxiety about the likelihood of fleas, I curled around her, grateful for some warmth.

A cataclysmic deluge the next morning threatened our chances of flying out. Akunai and I sat glumly under the eaves of the radio-operator's hut watching the rain. The radio operator had gone *wokabaut* looking for a missing piglet, and had taken the keys with him. The occasional villager sauntered up and sat down, offering a little *kaukau* or some words of wisdom. They would tut at the rain as if it were a personal grievance.

"Taim nogut. Bigpela ren na klaut. Big balus i no kam dawn. Samtaim no kam sikispela, sevenpela de samting."

There were many people waiting for *kago*. The last plane had landed five days ago. Supplies in the tradestore were running low and a team of seismic geologists were a week overdue. As one villager put it, the chances were only 'so-so'. I began to understand the desire for a road.

Hours passed. Even a glimmer of sunshine brought no hope. We sat on, interminably waiting. When the plane finally appeared it took us all by surprise. The distant drone of its engine might have been another hallucination. But when its shadow fell for a second or two on a bank of drifting cloud, everyone leapt to their feet.

"Balus i kam nau!"

There were whoops and shrieks as villagers converged on the airstrip. Overhead, the plane buzzed invisibly, assessing the landing, and then it appeared like a mosquito over the end of the runway. It crabbed awkwardly towards us, wobbling in the crosswind, bobbing along on pockets of air, and then sank triumphantly onto the gravel. A round of spontaneous applause broke out from the crowd. The Twin Otter spun on a sixpence barely inches from the end of the runway.

A tall Papuan wearing pilot's shorts and short sleeves unfolded himself from the cockpit and sprang to the ground. Some of the villagers reached forward to click fingers and pat him on the back. He walked coolly round to the baggage lockers to unpack his *kago*. There were boxes of chicken crackers and dried noodle soup, tins of corned beef, dripping, *tinpis* and cooking oil, net bags full of cabbages, some metal cases of seismic equipment, boxes of day-old chicks, the village mailbag and a new gas primer for the mission station. An added requirement of PNG pilots, it seemed, was to have the strength of Charles Atlas.

Akunai and I were weighed on a pair of bathroom scales and then put to work assembling our seats in the hold. The tool box was full of dead cockroaches. Another passenger launched himself into the co-pilot's seat. He was wearing a baseball cap for the trip and shook our hands like a team-mate psyching up for the big game.

"*Taim nogut,*" he said, nodding at the darkening sky. As the pilot began flicking switches, he stretched an avuncular arm around the pilot seat and watched with approval. "*Em nau,*" he said.

The pilot shouted "Clear prop!" outside the window and waited for the crowd to withdraw before turning the ignition. The propellers choked into action, hiccupping as they gathered speed and then spun into equilibrium. We lurched forward over the uneven ground, the aluminium framework creaking and judder-ing to an imaginary holding point at the top of the airstrip, which was little more than a steep muddy slope fortified with a sprin-kling of gravel and crash barriers of yellow clay. There were no flags or lights or large white numbers, nothing like a control tower or even radio contact. Just a soggy windsock.

Around us, the mountains dictated a rapid ascent and steep, banking turns. The runway itself was less than four hundred yards long. The weather was closing in again as we spun dizzily off the end of the runway to climb up and around and out of the surrounding mountains. Within seconds we had hit the bank of cloud that had been descending onto the airstrip. Akunai looked pale and worried in the sheen of white light inside the aircraft. Somewhere outside, there lurked mountain peaks as invisible and treacherous as reefs in a dark sea. The man with the baseball cap was leaning into the pilot's seat and clutching it, as if he might pierce the upholstery with his fingers.

Then suddenly, like a ship reaching smooth waters around a breaker, we hit sunlight and the steady, blue calm of clear skies. The man in the baseball cap turned round and gave us a thumbs up. The vision outside the cockpit was as uplifting as a Tiepolo ceiling. The peaks of some mountains sat like islands above the clouds and we cruised along between them like appreciative sightseers.

But there was barely time to sit back and relax. After twenty minutes – a length of time that belied the geographical barriers between Pimaga and Mendi – we were descending again, search-ing for an approach to the Southern Highlands capital. The pilot had taken off his sunglasses and was peering this way and that, tipping the plane to check his blind spots.

"When we go down," he warned, "it'll have to be fast. You

may feel some pressure in your ears. Just hold your nose and keep on blowing until we level out. We'll be fine."

And then we fell, diving through the cloud with searing speed, the air like rocks in our ears and the eerie, light-headed sensation that comes from almost losing the contents of your stomach. Like astronauts returning to the atmosphere we levelled out low above the Mendi Valley, skimming over familiar long, low bush houses and casuarinas, *kaukau* gardens and tarmac roads. There were cars and trucks below us, beetling along indifferently – the first traffic we had seen in days. And big buildings – banks, presumably, and supermarkets. The spell of Kutubu was broken.

Busybee was waving frantically from the other side of the perimeter fence. He was overwhelmed to see us.

"Hello, hello," he said, clasping my hand in both of his, all traces of shyness overcome by the moment. "My friends, good friends. Welcome, welcome."

We walked together towards the truck that had waited untouched for days by the airstrip. And then Busybee was off in top-speed Kamano, recounting the incidents of his journey from Porgera: the Engan driver, the long days in the Baptist Guesthouse, the strange meals and the even stranger people.

"He says he thought we were never coming back," said Akunai, when Busybee finally paused for breath. "He thought we'd died out there. And then when they said no planes could get to us because of the weather, he thought he was going to spend the rest of his life in Mendi. It's made him feel very ill. He hasn't spoken to anyone for days. He couldn't find one person from Goroka – just strange faces everywhere."

Driving around town to find petrol and food, it was difficult to see what the people of Lake Kutubu could ever gain from a road to Mendi. Gangs of itinerant workers hung gloomily around the main drag. The shops were boarded up and barred like the shops in Hagen. The tins on the supermarket shelves were rusting and past their use-by date; bags of rice crawled with weevils. There was an air of truculent resignation about the place, another no-man's land of empty promises.

As we drove through the outskirts of Mendi, striking out for the Hailans Haiwe with the engine coughing from the effects of black-market petrol, our spirits began to rise. We reached countryside and opened all the windows. Busybee leaned his head out and shouted, "*Gutbai* Mendi! *Gude* Goroka! We are Goroka men going home!", and we sped on our way, leaving paradise and purgatory behind us.

Late that evening, several hours after curfew, we arrived in Goroka. Busybee and Akunai were determined not to spend another night in foreign parts, so we had flogged the truck to within an inch of its life. The prospect of *rascals* after dark had been too much for tired minds to contemplate. We were lucky; several other cars were stopped by roadblocks and robbed on the Simbu border only hours after we had passed.

Busybee's house was quiet and in darkness, but as we drove away I saw the lights come on and the little *skulmankis* run out to meet him. Despite his exhaustion, I knew he would be awake until the early hours relating his experiences to a circle of disbelieving *wantoks*.

Akunai and I drove on in silence. We were spinning and speechless from the distance we had travelled that day, but we were also weighed down by all we had seen. The Eastern Highlands had so far felt only the tremors of the earth-shattering changes that would flow on from Porgera and Hides. But we had witnessed the cracks that would soon spread across the country. We both needed time to recover, and parted with scarcely a word, to deal with our demons alone.

CHAPTER 11

Mercenaries, Missionaries and Misfits

The Lutheran Guesthouse in Goroka was a forbidding building in a barbed-wire compound next to the church. It was where I installed myself while we planned our next trip and Akunai caught up with work and *wantoks*. It was worse than being back at school. The house master was a grumpy ex-minister from Australia with a chip on his shoulder and a nasty way of creeping up on you in the corridor. Only his wife, who wore A-line skirts and Scholl sandals, surpassed him in the open-hostility stakes. She made it quite plain from first acquaintance that she had exhausted her patience somewhere in the Australian outback and wasn't likely to find any hidden reserves in Papua New Guinea. An aggrieved sign on the doorbell in her hand read 'Press ONCE only!'.

The walls throughout the clapboard mission house were painted an institutional cream and illuminated by strip lights. The place was spotlessly clean, the blank walls relieved only by religious or sentimental posters and handwritten notices:

'No intoxicating liquor allowed on the premises'
'No chewing of betelnut'

'No noise after 10 pm'
'Dinner at 6 pm'
'Breakfast at 7.15 am'
'Wake-up bell 6.30'
'Use the bathmat'
'Use hot water sparingly'
'No pets or unmarried couples'

On a table in the hall was a spread of leaflets on AIDS and sexually transmitted diseases, guaranteed to make the reader scratch with guilt and alarm, and a pamphlet in pidgin depicting a black devil and a white angel wrestling over a man's heart.

I shared the women's dormitory with two German tourists and an American missionary from Lae who was recovering from a bout of malaria. Their beds were made like straightjackets. The reading matter on their bedside tables was telling: an Australian *Elle*, a German Agatha Christie, an LL Bean mail-order catalogue and a *Gut Nius* pocket Bible. They knelt together beside their beds at night to pray, and the American would turn off the light at exactly nine o'clock. "God bless. Sleep tight."

Their self-satisfied air of good will was shattered one morning by the arrival of a veteran missionary from Okapa.

"Get a move on, you monkey," he shouted at a young national trailing behind him with a couple of heavy suitcases, "and give Mom a hand with those ledgers."

He spotted me gaping at him from the lounge. "Gee, these young blackfellas can be slow as a fly swimmin' through molasses," he said, and extended his hand. "Chuck Morganstern's the name, baptisin's my game. Pleased to meet you."

Chuck was in his early seventies and had been a servant of the Lord in Papua New Guinea on and off for thirty years. His face was weather-beaten and tanned like buckskin, and a pair of clear blue eyes twinkled mischievously as if trying to share the joke. He filled the hallway like a bear.

A spindly, squeaky-clean lad followed him into the lounge. This was Billy's second week in PNG and he was all gung-ho and garrulous about it. He'd never been further than the west coast of the States before, and that had been only for a week-end church convention; Papua New Guinea was real neat. Before I could beat a retreat, he dragged me through the door to meet Mom, explaining that, in their role as godparents, Chuck and Martha Morganstern liked everyone who had come to know the Lord through them to call them Mom and Dad. A tiny, broken figure was shuffling through the hallway with a holdall in her hand. She was bent almost double, the top of her spine rising in a hump behind her head as the result of a medical accident that had broken her back in eight places and crippled her for life. She had struggled on for thirty years in PNG, battling against arthritis in every joint, walking the long handmade roads to the mission station because it hurt her too much to ride in the truck.

"This little lady has a place carved for her in heaven," cried Billy. "Here, let me carry that for you, Ma. I want you to meet a new friend who's staying here at the guesthouse."

Martha Morganstern looked up, her blue eyes swimming beneath pencilled black eyebrows. Her hair was thinning and yellow, and her face, pinched with exhaustion, was clumsily made up with blue eye shadow and smudged lipstick.

"Nice to know you," she said, vaguely curious at the sight of a stranger. "I hope we'll be breaking bread with you at the evening meal tonight. The Lord throws us together and it's up to us to get on with it."

Billy escorted her into her room and came bouncing back to cut off my exit. "You know, the Lord is so strong in her, it gives me strength just to be with her, sharing in her pain." He sat me down in a chair and fetched two cups of tea from the urn.

"Tell me," he said, his eyes glistening with enthusiasm, "how did you come to know the Lord?"

———

Later, in the relative sanity of the Air Niugini travel agency, I tried to sort out two tickets to Irian Jaya. It was a welcome reprieve from the guesthouse. But at the end of the day, with our passports safely dispatched to the Indonesian embassy in Moresby, there was no alternative and I slunk back for supper. A few minutes later Chuck walked in.

"Hell, it's good to be back in Goroka. There's nothing better than a good hot shower and a good hot dinner to look forward to."

He barely glanced at his newspaper before he leaned forward and addressed me again.

"You familiar with this crazy country? You know it gets to you. Like a woman. Bugs the hell out of you at times. Can't live with it, can't live without it."

He shot me a mischievous, almost flirtatious, look. "Keeps you on your toes like a good woman too. Hell, you have to lock your mouth when you're asleep or these *rascals* will have your back teeth out 'fore you know it."

He smiled wryly at the thought. "Yep. You gotta keep your wits about you and beat a few butts if you want to gain some respect. Action speaks louder than words here, that's what counts with these people."

"How do you go about converting people?" I dared to ask. He thought for a moment.

"You have to forget about the loving kindness of the Lord," he said. "Here, that's seen as weakness. Strength is what they admire. The best way to bring them the Lord – and this was taught me by the missionary before me – is to put one hand round the back of the head," and so saying, he spread out his fingers and held an imaginary face up to his, "and slap them round the cheeks," and his other hand swiped through the air. "Then tell them that Jesus loves them. That's what they understand."

I stared at him in disbelief. I doubted that Akunai's father would have stood for that.

"These people are like children," he persisted. "They have to be shown the way with good, sound discipline. They don't stop at nothing to get one over on you. And, hey, I'm allergic to arrows. You have to defend yourself around here, make no mistake about it."

He leant forward, glancing around to make sure the coast was clear, and pulled up a trouser leg. "This is one of my best friends," he whispered, pulling out a bone-handled switchblade from the elastic in his sock. "Won't go anywhere without it."

He slipped it back in his sock and relaxed.

"That's nothing – I've got a Mace canister and a 120,000-volt stun gun in my suitcase upstairs. And then, of course, there's my best buddy," he said, laying his hand across his heart. I thought for a moment that he had returned to the world of religious symbolism and was referring to his soul or his conscience, to Christ within the Man or some oath of allegiance. Instead, he opened up his jacket and revealed a pistol in his inside breast pocket.

"That's a .22 Dillinger," he said proudly. "Haven't had the need to use it yet, thank the Lord, but there've been some pretty close calls. Why, only last week, after we picked Billy up from the airstrip, we were stopped by a bunch of *rascals* who'd felled a tree across the road. And this guy was asking for money. 'No way, Jose,' I said, *'rot no bilong yu – rot bilong gavman',* then I sorta accidentally gave him a close look at my pistol, pushed a pidgin Bible in his hands and told him to get that log the hell out of my way, which he did. You see – just like children – they respect authority."

There is a saying in PNG that there are only three types of ex-pat – mercenary, missionary and misfit – and it occurred to me as I listened to the rantings of the Reverend Morganstern that I had just met the incarnation of all three: a sort of unholy trinity.

Martha crept into the room on paper-thin legs. "You cussing again?" she said irritably.

"No, dear," said Chuck, winking at me and playing the hen-pecked husband as he ostentatiously gave her his seat. "If it wasn't for Martha showing me the way back in '56, I'd still be a good-fer-nuthin' hoodlum in New York City. That's all I did in them days – drink and gamble and get into fights. Before I knew the loving kindness of the Lord. Used to be a marine, too, in the Second World War, out here in the Pacific. You see some nasty things in war. Martha and the good Lord gave me the first peace I'd ever known."

Chuck lit up with the arrival of the shy young national I had seen him order about earlier that day. He smiled and slipped past us to the table to read the *Ragbi Lig Nius*.

"He's a sweet boy, Rinkio," Chuck said laughing, "when he's asleep that is. Although sometimes, when he gets out of hand, I have to crack him on the nut," and he rapped his knuckle on the wooden arm of his chair. "Do you know, their heads are as hard as wood – they hardly feel a thing? It's the shock of it that keeps them in line – ain't that right, Rinkio?"

Rinkio looked up from his reading as if he were tired of being disturbed. Chuck continued regardless. "He won't take a room here – prefers to sleep in the truck. He'll just about take his meals with us, but it took him a while to get used to that even."

Rinkio and another young man were being trained by the Morgansterns to take over the mission; he was twenty-three years old.

"We're real proud of him, Mother and me. Billy is teaching him music so he can conduct his own choir one day. We took him with us back to Honolulu a few years ago to educate him at mission school and he did real well. He's a smart kid."

From the hallway a bell sounded for dinner. The landlady from hell steamed in and set about passing dishes from the hatch in the kitchen to the table. The German girls appeared. Billy came rushing in, breathless and full of himself, having just completed a fifteen-page letter to his girlfriend. I had the sinking feeling some of it might describe his potential new convert from England.

"*Kaukau*," said Chuck, receiving a dish of sweet potatoes. "That's just what I want to see more of. Rinkio is about the only person round here who doesn't ever get tired of it. He'll eat it till it's coming out his ears. We call him the PK Kid – pumpkin and *kaukau*," he guffawed, "ain't that right, son?"

"I can't see the good in it," complained Billy, "seems to me there's no nutritional value in *kaukau* at all."

Quite unexpectedly, Rinkio paused mid-forkful and lifted his head. "*Kaukau* has plenty of nutrients in it," he said in an even, American accent, "it's full of vitamin A. And as a carbohydrate it's an excellent energy producer."

"You heard the boy," laughed Chuck, "get stuck in and stop complaining." Then he turned back to me.

"Always carry a bottle of alcohol concentrate with you wherever you go," he advised. "Because sometimes, especially in my business, you end up shaking hands with people filthier than some hobo lying on a New York sidewalk. Then, if there's no soap and clean water available, you can disinfect yourself and you won't catch some God-awful disease."

I felt embarrassed for Rinkio. Until he had spoken, I had no idea how good his English was. But Rinkio was calmly helping himself to seconds of chicken and, amazingly, appeared not to mind.

I was curious to know how many 'children' Chuck had converted.

"We have between twelve and fourteen thousand people in our area," said Chuck, reluctant to be distracted from his ravings.

"And how many of those are now Christian?" I persisted.

Chuck was noticeably irritated. "I'll tell you when I get to heaven," he said.

It was Billy who obliged with an answer. "We have on average two to three hundred children of the Lord in church every Sunday," he said, eager to be included in the conversation. But he was cut short. The return on a twenty-seven-year investment was clearly disastrous and Chuck was not going to sit by and discuss the measure of his success (or lack of it). Wiping his mouth self-consciously on his napkin and drawing back his chair, he addressed the table.

"If you'll excuse us, it's been a tiring day. Martha, dear, I think we should put you to bed and get you some rest." He helped her up from the table and steered her feeble body towards the door. It was a successful moment of pathos and the dinner table fell silent. It was only when they had left the room that conversation resumed.

The dishes were cleared away and slowly people wandered off to bed or to read. I found myself alone at the table with Rinkio, who had reopened his magazine.

"So you're going to become a missionary?" I asked, offering him a cup of coffee from the urn.

"I dunno," he answered. "I want to be a marine like Dad. I know he wants me to stay in the church, and I'll finish my education and my training. But I'd really like to go back to the States and sign up."

Rinkio's education seemed, ironically, to have backfired. The young Highlander had been seduced not by Chuck's ranting and ravings as a Christian, but by the very life that the missionary was trying, vainly, to put behind him.

"Dad's shown me how to use all sorts of guns and pistols," said Rinkio, "how to wrestle and use a knife. He really knows about weapons. And he's taught me how to ride a motorcycle and drive a car.

"I have my own gun now, though he doesn't know about it. Mom wouldn't let me keep it if she knew. One of my *wantoks* escaped from prison here in Goroka with a policeman's gun. He got me bullets, too. I'm getting real good at handling it. One day I'll show Dad how much my shooting's improved. Then maybe he'll help me join the marines."

I slipped quietly into the darkness of my bedroom that night, strangely comforted by Rinkio's single-minded ambition. Like the rest of the Fore people, he would not be terrorised into knowing the Lord, even by such a charismatic advocate as the Reverend Morganstern. He would rise to the opportunities the church could offer without compromising his own independence of spirit. God had liberated him from tribal life, but he was still a warrior at heart.

We were summoned by bells at seven the next morning. I could hear Chuck downstairs making his impact on the world.

"Rinkio, you monkey," he was shouting. "Get your lazy ass over here. You forgotten we're leaving this morning? Where've you put my keys? Billy, for God's sake put down that pen. This is no time for writing love letters . . . Where is everyone? I'll give them ten minutes before I say grace."

I made it downstairs with only seconds to spare before Chuck addressed the Almighty. After breakfast, I decided to make my escape. "Goodbye, Reverend," I said, "have a good trip back to Okapa."

"Where you off to next, young lady?" he asked, searching his pockets for his card.

"Irian Jaya."

"Well, you can tell those Indonesians from me," he said, with the old glint in his eye, "if they ever dare cross the 141st parallel – and I can tell you, one day they'll try – they'll have me and my children to reckon with. The good Lord is no stranger to guerrilla warfare and those Muslims won't know what's hit them if they cross the border into PNG. Tell them that." I had to smile, so eager did he seem for the scrap.

"Here's my card," he added, "and a few mementos to take with you on your journey."

He handed me a yellow plastic key ring with a bird of paradise on one side and 'Papua New Guinea – Independence 1975' on the other; a leaflet on homosexuality, drug abuse and the Catholic conspiracy; and a glossy colour postcard of Martha and himself taken in Honolulu. Martha was looking startled and Chuck had his arm cradled protectively around her shoulders, beaming a bright, mischievous smile. Above their heads ran the legend 'Pray for Us', and beneath: 'Chuck & Martha Morganstern,

Missionaries to Papua New Guinea and the World'.

In the hallway, I said a much cooler farewell to Billy, who was licking down an envelope ready for posting. It was so much more difficult to like someone who was bloodless than someone who was bloodthirsty.

"You probably won't see us again. You certainly won't see Dad," he said.

I was confused.

"He's only got a few weeks to live. Didn't you know? The doctor in Honolulu diagnosed liver cancer two months ago. That's why he's come here so soon after the last trip. He wants to die in Papua New Guinea."

Akunai seemed grateful for the break while we waited for our passports to arrive back from Port Moresby. His office was in chaos. The premier had been on a bender while we were away and some of his lieutenants had thrown up in Akunai's car. Akunai's desk was a mountain of paper – mostly from departments other than his own. But he was also still reeling from the last trip. He needed to come back down to earth, he said, before taking off again.

"You Europeans do too much travelling," he argued. "We're still getting used to all this hopping about from place to place. You travel like you eat. Very fast, always on the move, with no time for digesting. I've got to let my stomach settle from all those helicopters and yabbies and crazy warriors on the warpath before I can think about Irian Jaya and millions of Indonesians."

The Lutheran Guesthouse, though, was beginning to seem like a prison sentence. Since the departure of the Morgansterns, normality had resumed with choking monotony – ringing bells, prayers and platitudes, nit-picking and pleasantries were the order of every day; meal times were becoming interminable. Like a passenger tempted to pull the emergency cord on a slow train between stations, I was aggravated into taking drastic action. As guiltily as an adulterer or alcoholic, I slipped out of the guesthouse and telephoned an ex-pat called Duncan Jones.

A friend of mine had given me Duncan's number. It came with a government health warning, and it took no time at all to see why. An ex-Vietnam chopper pilot, he lived resolutely by his own rules; he was a self-made millionaire and the proud owner of islands off the coast.

"I'll pick you up in two minutes – drop everything you're doing, if it's legal that is, and be ready to be swept off your feet," he said. He didn't ask how I came to have his number.

"What'll you be wearing – anything? Tell you what, I won't look out for you – you look out for me. I'll be the one with no hair."

I put the phone down, dazed. "Do you know Duncan Jones?" I asked the telephonist, after a while.

"Duncan," he giggled nervously, "*em i man bilong maus-wara.*"

"What does that mean?" I asked

"It means I'm a windbag," said a voice from behind me, "or 'full of mouth water'. Verbal diarrhoea we'd call it. Or 'bullshit' – pardon my French."

I thought he had been joking about the hair but Duncan was as bald as an egg. He was tall and thickly built – a kind of prepossessing Humpty Dumpty. He swaggered in, wearing shorts and thongs, with the air of a man used to having his own way. If we had been in a saloon, he would have swung through the doors twirling pistols in both hands. As it was, his reputation as a big shot in town needed no reinforcement. The girl at reception smiled flirtatiously and the simpering telephonist ducked his head out of provocation's way.

"Duncan Disorderly," he introduced himself, transfixing me with riveting eye contact. "I think we know each other well enough for a kiss hello. Two please, French style."

He wasn't flattered by my hesitation. "Don't worry," he said, "women are completely sexless to me – you're not a 'he' or a 'she' – you're just an 'it'. Until I sleep with you, that is."

He led me, dumbfounded, to his pick-up and drove the three minutes to the Aeroclub on the edge of the airstrip without drawing breath.

It was six-thirty and the club was already doing good business. Raucous reports of male laughter issued from the bar as we approached. My heart sank as I steeled myself for the barrage that predictably greeted us at the door.

"Nice one, Duncan."

"How come you get all the pretty girls?"

"Must be the shampoo he uses."

"Don't trust him, sweetheart. He's just a pretty face, you know."

"Oh, I dunno, Tim. Beneath that soft exterior beats a heart – I think."

Duncan grinned and guided me forward. "I'd like you to meet a young lady from England. England, mind you, so mind your P's and Q's."

One of his mates offered to get the drinks and sidled his way through the crowd to the end of the room. Screwed to the wall next to the bar was a helicopter seat, complete with safety belts. "You might need that, later on," said another of Duncan's friends, "if Duncan has his way. That's the worse-for-wear chair. We put people in it when they can't stand up any more. But it doesn't give you an excuse to stop drinking."

There were very few nationals in the bar and only a couple of women – wives of pilots based in Goroka. The room was full of smoke and the boom of men forgetting their responsibilities. Most of them would be up at dawn for another day's work cheating the mountains and the weather. Some might be destined for Porgera. Several of them would be flying on paracetamol and bicarbonate of soda.

I asked Duncan what had brought him to PNG in the first place.

"Put it like this," he said, taking a long swig from his pint, "when you've spent several years of your youth being shot at in enemy territory over virgin jungle in some Godforsaken part of the world, you find it a bit difficult to settle down in Coronation Street. Some of the guys here served in 'Nam and they're probably the best pilots in the world. Put them in the cockpit of an airliner or a crop-sprayer and they'll go bloody loco. Where's the challenge, the adrenalin, the skill in that? You might as well be a bloody machine. Fuck the money – s'cuse my French – you gotta do something that keeps the little grey cells alive and kicking."

His friends were in agreement, and hung onto his words as if he were articulating the essence of their existence. Some more men pushed through the front door and slapped Duncan on the back on their way to the bar.

"Not that flying helicopters is a glamorous business out here. Sometimes it can be rank. You know, one of my first jobs was as a body collector. All in all I suppose I've collected fifty bodies out of plane crashes in PNG – although you can't really call them bodies after they've hit the ground at over one hundred and fifty miles an hour. And after a couple of weeks – which is how long it can take before you find it – the body can be crawling with maggots."

He barely disguised the pleasure he took in describing it.

"You just have to pick up as many pieces as you can find, maggots and all, dump them in a body bag and take them with you. Jesus, the stench can be terrible. Ever smelt rotting human flesh? You just can't get rid of it." He took another long draught of beer. "Once, I had to ferry the body of an ex-pat who had died in a plane crash back to Cairns. But he'd been dropped off in a village for me to collect and the villagers had just left the bag lying out in the sun for two days – can you believe it? By the time I got to it, the whole thing had inflated with gas like a zeppelin. When they carried it over to the helicopter there was this slushing sound.

"Now that really did stink. When I got back to base, I just put it on the tarmac and said, 'That's it. It's all yours – I'm having nothing more to do with it. You can take it down to Cairns. I'm not spending another minute with this bag of soup'. Want another drink?"

I downed the remains of my beer and obediently handed over the glass.

"Thatta girl," said Duncan, and headed off for the bar.

The noise in the bar was like a pub on a Saturday night. But it was midweek in Goroka. Nobody was strapped in the chair yet but it wouldn't be long before there were several contenders. Standing on my own I felt more than a little self-conscious; Duncan seemed to have disappeared. Then suddenly, out of nowhere, a great snarling animal leapt at my leg and bit me on the calf. I shrieked with surprise and fell backwards, knocking into a table; this triggered a sudden silence from all corners of the room, followed by roars of mortifying laughter.

"Gets 'em every time," laughed Duncan, getting up from all fours on the floor, "my rabid-dog trick. Didn't scare you, did I?" He was grinning with pleasure, his face slightly pink from the heat of the room and the exertion of his prank. Someone came over with more beer. My half-pint glass had been swapped for a pint.

"Now, where was I," said Duncan, "before you were so rudely interrupted? Oh, yes. What was it like when I first landed up in PNG – I remember. Well, there was this flu epidemic in the Highlands – 1969 to 1970 – and I was recruited on a vaccination programme, to fly medics to areas around Oksapmin.

"I don't know if you've ever seen any of these guys, but in those days they were all wearing penis gourds and precious little else; they still do on the other side of the border, I believe. I was given a syringe and told to jab them all in the bums. There were thousands of them, all queuing up for their jab. And there was one guy who had an Eveready battery on his willy – can you believe it? Quite appropriate really, he looked like a bit of a goer. How it didn't fall off I just don't know. Maybe the altitude.

"And the women. Wow, that was something. All those beautiful bodies in tiny little grass things. I swear that's where they invented the mini-skirt. I used to try and blow their skirts up with my down-draught but the damn things never budged an inch. Amazing."

With yet more beers the conversation turned to the night ahead and suggested venues for the continuation of the party. Haunted by the thought of my landlady I made my excuses and Duncan offered to drop me back. We screeched to a halt outside the guesthouse and he dropped me by the gate like a schoolgirl returning late from a day out.

"Keep in touch now," said Duncan Disorderly. "It's always good to see new faces – specially the pretty ones. Rubby noses, kiss, kiss," and so saying he leant across, kissed me on both cheeks and shook his nose against mine like some overgrown, bald Eskimo. I prayed my landlady was not watching from behind her net curtains, and bolted for the door.

CHAPTER 12

Arapela Kantri

Vanimo was an exotic anticlimax after being in the Highlands for a few weeks. The unassuming port on the north coast, nineteen miles from the Irian Jaya border, was bright and calm, with meandering rivers and wide expanses of sugar and copra. There was none of the turbulence of trapped weather systems, no mist or clouds or drizzle or dew. Despite its beauty, the atmosphere in the town was disappointingly flat. People strolled around the streets as if on an island in the Carribean. No one looked over their shoulder for *rascals*.

The only way to enter Irian Jaya from Papua New Guinea was from Vanimo. Our passports had been returned from the Indonesian embassy in Moresby with an indecipherable page of script inside them. But the visa didn't permit us to walk, drive or sail across what is still referred to in PNG as West Irian. We had to fly – not in a light aircraft either, but in a full-sized international Air Niugini Boeing.

Akunai had again said goodbye to his family in Goroka and was clearly missing the moral support of Busybee. In the eyes of his *wantoks*, he was not simply travelling to the western part of the Highlands: he was embarking on a journey to Asia. *Arapela kantri* they called it – another country. Papua New Guinea had erased all memory of its other half.

Akunai had no idea what to expect. He had come dressed for the journey wearing a 'Cairns, Australia' T-shirt: "So they don't think I'm from PNG. I don't want an arrow in my chest as soon as I arrive." His only luggage was a seisal *bilum*, sparingly packed with a camera and a new Wilbur Smith novel.

"I couldn't run away from a battle if I was carrying a *ruksak* like yours," he said. "And we can use the string from my *bilum* if we need a tourniquet."

I wasn't sure if he was joking.

The Boeing was a floating hotel after the Cessnas and Otters and Bandeirantes buzzing around the Highlands. But only six of the seventy-six seats were occupied. We all sat together towards the front, like passengers in an empty bus. Our companions were a Papua New Guinean diplomat and his wife, and two of their staff. The flight attendant welcomed us on board and announced a flying time of nine minutes. As we took off over Vanimo, people walking along the beach looked up and waved. Akunai waved back at the last sight of home. We turned in a slow, deliberate arc over the foothills and headed along the coast for the border.

Almost as soon as we found altitude we began to descend. Half-drunk cups of coffee and unopened biscuits were whisked away, tray-tables were stowed and we were advised, even before the seatbelt sign had been switched off, to make sure we were buckled in for landing. Beneath us, not surprisingly, the terrain had hardly changed. The sea still glittered silver and blue under the afternoon sun. We passed low over the feathery breasts of sago palms on the same foothills and along the shores of familiar lakes and lagoons.

But we touched down in a different country. There were military police on guard at the entrance to the terminal. The airport thronged with passengers, relatives, ground staff, drivers, officials: slender brown figures with clean-shaven faces and straight black hair. There wasn't another white or black face to be seen. While our passports were stamped, we were stormed by people, pressing in from all sides. They jostled and nudged with a boorishness that would have caused a punch-up in PNG. Akunai was clearly rattled. They pressed their faces up to his, clung to his clothes and prodded him for attention.

"I don't speak your language," Akunai repeated several times. "I can't understand you."

"Change money, change money."

"Good price rupiahs."

"What are they doing?" asked Akunai, helplessly.

We were ripped off by a black-market moneychanger who conducted his business behind a pillar in the entrance hall. The banks were closed and he had us over a barrel.

"No dollar?" he asked. He handed over a bundle of filthy pink notes – two hundred rupiah to the kina, instead of the bank price of two thousand. Akunai was mesmerised by the length of the nail on his little finger, which flashed ostentatiously as he flicked through his notes.

The air outside caught us by surprise with the aroma of clove cigarettes and spicy food, a whiff of cheap aftershave, the smell of commerce. We saw our first nationals, explaining themselves to an official. "*Monin, nau,*" said Akunai automatically as we passed them. They turned and stared blankly.

"Did you see that?" cried Akunai. "They were speaking Indonesian – and they can't even understand pidgin."

We were herded towards a smart new Honda in the car park

by our walking *bureau de change*. "This taxi my friend. Give you excellent, very good price to Jayapura."

Around the parking lot were statues of Highland warriors – kitsch, cheap effigies with fake necklaces, plastic feather head-dresses, spears and grass skirts, but enough to spark off a thrill of recognition in Akunai.

"Look – they're wearing kina shells. They've got *kundu* drums and shields like ours. But where's the real thing? Where are all the nationals?"

There were cluttered settlements on the road to Jayapura, little shanty towns resting on stilts at the edge of Lake Sentani. There were workshops and junkyards and road stalls and light-indus-trial units. But there was no sign of the indigenous population. There were no pigs on the road, no one carried *bilums*. Where cranky, overcrowded PMVs would have plied their trade on the other side of the border, here there were spanking-new Mitsubishis and Toyota minibuses. There were cars and vans and motorbikes in a profusion with which even expatriate Port Moresby could not compete.

We sped around the bends above the lake, past billboards of Jakarta and an effigy of a policeman with his hand held up to slow us down.

"That's where these people should be – Java or Sumatra or somewhere," said Akunai, with sudden venom. "From the plane, I thought, 'Look, it's a big, developing city. There should be lots of nationals working down there with houses and good money, building up their country'. But there's no one. Just hundreds and thousands of Indonesians trying to turn New Guinea into another piece of Indonesia."

We passed an army barracks, then a police barracks, then a detention centre. At last we arrived at Jayapura: a shambles of corrugated iron, concrete and cement, punctuated here and there by the rusting helmet of a mosque. A stench of raw sewage blasted through the windows as we emerged onto the main drag. Open drains ran down the side of the road and a dead dog lay halfway across one of them, creating a blockage of rubbish and silt. The centre of town was almost solid with traffic. Bicycles and motorbikes swerved about in a cacophony of bells and horns. We had reached a bottleneck, and cars jammed together with impatience to get through. Our driver leant on his horn for an impotent twenty seconds. Passers-by whistled and shouted and wandered through the traffic, contributing to the chaos. The quiet streets of Goroka were a million miles away.

In 1910, when the Dutch chose a site for Jayapura, or Hollandia as it was then called, the beauty of the bay had been one of their chief considerations. The other motive governing their choice was the desire to have the Dutch capital in New Guinea right up against the German territory in the north-east.

The population numbered a few thousand until, with the outbreak of the Second World War, Hollandia found itself the target of military operations in the Pacific. The Japanese made it their base, sweeping aside a meagre Dutch defence and establishing the Sentani airstrip. Then the Allies under General MacArthur recaptured Hollandia after a dramatic amphibious attack and the town exploded with a quarter of a million American and Australian personnel.

After the war, Hollandia shrank considerably again – to around seventeen thousand people. By then Indonesia was independent and the Dutch were fighting for West Irian as their last remaining possession in the East Indies. In an attempt to keep the territory from falling into Indonesian hands, they actually encouraged West Irian nationalism and made a concerted effort to prepare the indigenous people for independence, educating the elite at schools and universities back in Holland (just as the Australians later trained Papua New Guineans at Sogeri and Port Moresby University).

The West Irians fully expected to gain independence before PNG. They held themselves up as an example to their counterparts in the Australian Territory of Papua and New Guinea, and there was even talk of reuniting New Guinea one day, when both sides were independent.

But it was not to be. Indonesia, under its aggressive new President Sukarno, was burdened with economic problems and a burgeoning population. Sukarno sought to distract attention away from these domestic problems by fighting for West Irian; if successful, he would also secure a territory in which to resettle hundreds of thousands of peasant farmers from massively overpopulated areas in Indonesia.

In the end, Indonesia won the day. Alarmed by an outright attack by Indonesian armed forces on the Dutch in West Irian, the United States urged compromise. The last thing it wanted to see was Indonesia driven into the arms of the Soviet Union for military support. A so-called 'Act of Free Choice' was declared by the United Nations, whereby Indonesia was to administer West Irian on a trial basis for five years, after which time a plebiscite would decide whether the territory wished to remain Indonesian.

When the time came for the referendum in 1969, West Irian had been swamped with Indonesian migrant workers. The indigenous people had been intimidated into submission, gunned down by aircraft, burned from their villages and driven from their lands. Instead of a full-scale, democratic plebiscite, one thousand representatives were 'chosen' by the Indonesian administration to vote on behalf of their country. Not surprisingly, the decision was unanimous. West Irian was renamed Irian Jaya – 'Victorious Irian'; Hollandia became Sukarnopura and then Jayapura, and Indonesian settlers sent the city's population rocketing to its present two hundred and fifty thousand.

The only opposition to Indonesian rule came in the form of the Free Papua Movement, or the OPM (Organisasi Papua Merdeka) – a West Irian guerrilla force aiming to oust the Asian administration and establish independence. But the OPM was, by reputation, an ill-organised, ill-equipped, shambolic affair. Few of the campaigns it conducted ever achieved results and its various factions constantly fought amongst each other. Fearful of the military strength and unpredictable designs of Indonesia, Australia had long discouraged support for the movement, and PNG seemed to look on the OPM almost as an embarrassment.

The few West Irians in PNG – only several hundred or so – who had attained citizenship after managing to stay in the country for the statutory eight years kept an advisedly low profile. Other West Irians fleeing the Indonesian regime were held in refugee camps on the PNG side of the border in discreet, remote areas, and consistently repatriated. While the activities of the OPM were reported now and then in the PNG press, few Papua New Guineans had ever met a West Irian, let alone a Free Papua guerrilla.

We had picked our hotel in Jayapura at random from a guide-book. It was one of the most expensive, but it cost less than the cheapest hotel in Moresby. We had little time to spare in

Jayapura. Had we been able to buy our tickets and permits outside the country, we could have avoided it altogether and flown straight to the Highlands; but the vortex of bureaucracy drew us in as surely as it diverts any plans in Indonesia, whirling us from one dingy office to another through a nightmare performance of bank slips, police forms and travel agencies. Akunai seemed completely at sea.

Our major objective was to obtain a *surat jalan* – the travel permit that would allow us to fly to Wamena, the capital of the Baliem Valley up in the Central Highlands. We would have to carry this with us at all times for identification, show it at every village we visited in the valley and have it stamped and authorised anywhere we intended to spend the night. To Akunai, the restrictions were incredible.

"You mean they can move us on or tell us to turn back whenever they feel like it?" he asked a face behind a desk.

Just as the office was about to close we were granted our permits.

That evening, after dark, we went to find somewhere to eat. Akunai was disconcerted to see the town come alive so late. "This place is all back to front," he said. "Everything shuts in the afternoon, then they all come out at night. Don't they have any spirits to worry about?"

But the vision of the market by night was as entrancing as the spectacle by day had been depressing. Jayapura had been transformed. The streets had blossomed miraculously with hundreds of tiny food stalls hung with lanterns or bursting with electric light. There were open fires and barbeques, tended by sweaty stall owners flipping fish and corn cobs. In the privacy of shelters or beneath the convention of a single plastic sheet, families, couples, loners and children sat on benches over bowls of food.

The place was buzzing with chatter and sentimental music. The air was fragrant with woodsmoke and the savoury aromas of good cooking.

We sat down at a table covered with a flowery plastic table-cloth on which was placed a vase of plastic flowers. A little Chinese boy served us immediately, bringing spoons, two bowls of fish soup with lemon grass, and saucers of soy, chilli and peanut sauce. Akunai dipped distastefully into his bowl.

"Lucky Busybee isn't here," he said, "he'd starve to death."

I was woken next morning by the call to prayer from a nearby mosque. My head was still buzzing with the sound of uninter-rupted traffic. It was four-thirty and our plane was due to leave for the Highlands at seven.

Akunai was wide awake, fully dressed and waiting in the lobby with his *bilum* over his shoulder. We hailed a cab and headed for the airport. It was still dark but the town had been cleared of all the food stalls from the night before. A couple of trawlers were just returning to the docks and the tiny lights of fishing boats were bobbing up and down in the lagoons – something one would never see in Papua New Guinea.

"Look," said Akunai, "they're still looking for food at this time of night. Shows how many people these Indonesians are trying to feed."

After a burble of Indonesian love songs, John Lennon's 'Imagine' came on the taxi radio.

"Imagine all the people," Akunai laughed. "That's exactly what I'd like to forget."

Dawn was breaking at the airport. There were hundreds of passengers already gathered in the terminal, jostling with bags and boxes, bottles and tins and stacks of cooking pots. There was mayhem at customs control. People were waving their *surat jalans* at any official they could see. There were no queues, just a surging throng falling forward towards the customs desks and being driven back by uniformed police. We ebbed and flowed for an anxious hour and a half until we were admitted to the departure lounge with only fifteen minutes to spare.

We need not have hurried. Our plane to Wamena was delayed indefinitely. For hour upon hour we waited in the airport café, eating sticky rice cakes and drinking tea sweetened with half a cup of condensed milk. No official explanation was forthcoming over the Tannoy, but our estimated departure time was regularly given and it was always two hours away. It went without saying that this would never have been tolerated in Papua New Guinea. Akunai sat on, mutely celebrating aviation efficiency in his own country.

"It's not knowing what's going on that makes me nervous," he said at last. "There's no flight number on the boarding pass, no seat number, no name. We could be anyone going anywhere, we could just be forgotten. People seem to be anonymous in this country."

It was two in the afternoon when we were finally ushered onto the tarmac. The air was thick with the humidity of mid-afternoon. Only when we sped off the end of the runway, soaring on a wing tip over Lake Sentani, did Akunai allow himself a sigh of relief.

"Highlands here we come," he said longingly above the roar of the engines.

Within seconds the madding conurbations of Jayapura had surrendered to natural rainforest. As far as the eye could see, dense, undulating jungle held sway, broken only by the occasional muddy ribbon meandering in the oxbow lakes of a geography textbook.

"It's just like Enga Province," said Akunai, snapping frantically through his window, "or the Sepik."

After half an hour or so, the country began to change. Flickers of limestone could be seen amongst the trees, heralding the foothills of the Snow Mountains – the Indonesian end of the New Guinea range. Soon we were passing over cliffs and ravines, climbing ever higher to clear them. There were deep, spectacular ravines, spun with mist as deep as the Strickland Gorge in PNG.

An hour later we levelled out over the top of a ridge and began to descend into the magnificent Baliem Valley. Over half a century earlier, five years after the pioneering expedition of the Leahy brothers to the Hagen and Goroka valleys, the first white man to set eyes on Baliem had flown over this pass. An American naturalist, Richard Archbold, who had been sent on a joint-venture expedition by the Dutch administration and the American Museum of Natural History, had flown his seaplane into the largest remaining blank space on the map of New Guinea. He had soared over the indomitable limestone fortress we had just passed and discovered beneath him the largest and most fertile Highland valley in all New Guinea, home to a tribal population of fifty thousand.

From the air, the view was a postcard from PNG. The valley floor was spread out in a patchwork of gardens – faded where they lay fallow, luminous green where new crops sprouted. There were rows and copses of casuarinas for windbreaks and shade, and beneath the most substantial of these, as we glided down on our final approach, the thatched mushroom caps of village houses. Tiny dark figures were running into the clearings and waving up at the sound of our plane.

Chapter 13

Hailans Bilong West Irian

We touched down on an airstrip protected from trespassing children and pigs by a traditional wooden fence. Outside, on the tarmac, the fresh air was electrifying.

"We're in the Highlands!" cried Akunai in amazement, gazing up at the mountains on either side. "Back in the Highlands of PNG!"

The airport was swarming with Melanesians, who outnumbered the slight figures of the Indonesian airport staff and hotel owners. Most of the Melanesians were naked except for penis gourds, which jutted proudly from their groins. Some gourds were thin and pointed and reached to the chest; some were short and twisted, or curled against the hip like a pig's tail; some, mostly the younger men's, were big and fat and tubular like a length of drainpipe, strapped to the stomach with wide bands of colourful cloth. They were all held in position by threads from a spider's web twisted around the scrotum.

I anticipated some embarrassment from Akunai, but he was unabashed. The human body is only indecent when it is exposed to the wrong people in the wrong place. Here, penis gourds were as natural as kilts in Scotland or bikinis on Waikiki. Akunai was thrilled.

"I haven't seen penis gourds for years. Some people in West Sepik Province – around Oksapmin and Telefomin – still wear them, I think. But in Goroka Valley we haven't seen them for more than thirty years."

As soon as we were inside the airport terminal we were besieged by people, just as we had been in Jayapura. Most of the men with penis gourds held back, a little shy of the throng or perhaps anxious for the safety of their gourds in the melee. But there were also Melanesians in European dress, who, along with their Asian competitors, badgered us with recommendations: places to stay, treks, taxis, restaurants, tours. *"Vous restez ici, monsieur?" "Sprechen sie Deutsch?" "Speaking Inglis?"*

Akunai was taken aback by the uncharacteristic onslaught. "Highlanders should never be so forward," he muttered, as we were pushed through the doors onto the street. "Indonesia has taught them to be greedy."

But it was clear we would not get away without recruiting the services of someone, so, without much reflection, we opted for a small, eager Melanesian who had been hopping up and down at our side ever since we entered the building. He could have scored a winning goal in a PNG *ragbi* match, so thrilled was he to be chosen.

"Good choice, my friends, good choice. I'm very good guide, excellent guide," he said. "Name Niko. You come with me. Nearest hotel very nice. Thank you very *mux.*" He wore a shabby pair of slacks made from synthetic fibre and flared from the knee, a green T-shirt and a pair of cast-off track shoes from a former client. He steered us away from the airport and down the road towards the Nayak Hotel.

"You Africa man?" he asked Akunai.

Akunai shook his head. "No, I'm from Papua New Guinea."

There was a moment's stunned silence. Niko had stopped, frozen, in the middle of the road.

"Fafa-Noo-Guinea?" he repeated, thunderstruck. "Fafa-Noo-Guinea?"

"Yes," said Akunai, a little uncertainly.

Suddenly, Niko flung his arms around Akunai's waist. "My friend, my brother," he cried. There were tears in his eyes. "From Fafa-Noo-Guinea." He stood back to take another look and then looked at me as if to double check. He simply could not believe it.

Because Akunai seemed too disconcerted to speak, I told him we had just come from Vanimo and that Akunai lived in the Highlands of Papua New Guinea, in a valley just like the Baliem. Niko was holding Akunai's hand as if he would never let him go.

"You live in valley," he repeated. "In Highlands Fafa-Noo-Guinea."

Gently, he inclined his head and rested it against Akunai's chest like a child. Then he looked again in triumph at Akunai's face. "You face like us. You first time brother from Fafa-Noo-Guinea. One man from Africa come here to Wamena and he look like us. But he say no – he say he from other side of the world, too far away. From Nigeria. He is black like us," said Niko, pointing to his arm next to Akunai's, "but with big body. Too big for Dani people. We wait long time to see our brother. Now you come. Real Fafa-Noo-Guinea."

Bursting with his discovery, Niko gestured to a group of boys hanging around the entrance to the Nayak Hotel. In an excited garble, punctuated by 'Fafa-Noo-Guineas', he explained Akunai's provenance. The boys fell upon their new visitor with exclamations of surprise, patting him on the back, clasping his arms, touching his face. Akunai's instinctive discomfort at being the object of their attention was overcome by the thrill of the moment. Where he had anticipated an arrow in the back he was being received as a hero, and this came as a relief as much as an honour. Encouraged, as well, by the exuberance of his entourage and their warm-heartedness, he began to relax.

"This my friend and brothers," explained Niko to Akunai, "from my own village."

"In Papua New Guinea," said Akunai, "we call them *wantoks*. These are your *wantoks*."

"Yaaah!" cried Niko, beaming with pleasure, "*wantoks*."

Then an idea struck him. "Hey! you no stay in Indonesian *losmen*. You stay with your *wantoks*. Stay at my house. Yaah!"

Before we knew where we were, we were bundled into a minibus – an Indonesian *bemo* – with the rest of the crowd and heading out of town. Niko and I sat in the front seat, while Akunai was crammed in the back amongst his fans. The driver was an Indonesian, who sat solidly impervious to the celebratory mood of his passengers.

"You have *bemos* like this in Fafa-Noo-Guinea?" asked Niko, leaning over the back of the seat.

"Yes," said Akunai, "but we call them PMVs – Public Motor Vehicles. My cousin has one."

Niko gazed at him in surprise. "Your cousin driving *bemos*, driving BMPs? In Irian Jaya only Indonesians can buy *bemos*. Dani people cannot drive." He shook his head with pleasure and amazement. Already, this Papua New Guinean was living up to reputation. But suddenly Niko was struck with an unwelcome thought and his face clouded over with concern.

"You have *surat jalan?* We my friends spending night outside

Wamena, so we must going to police office for stamping *surat jalan,* yes."

The long hours waiting at Sentani airport had done nothing to lessen my prejudice against Indonesian authorities. The last thing I felt like doing was subjecting myself to more bureaucratic rigmarole.

"Let's not bother, Niko," I said. "They'll never know. Let's just go to your place and forget the police."

Niko looked horrified. Then slowly his expression began to melt into one of jubilant rebellion. "Yaah! my friends," he said at last. "We forget them policemen. We forget *surat jalan* – no problem." He clapped his hands with glee.

We were driving through Wamena town, past bungalows, offices and tourist guesthouses, or *losmen* – the exclusive property of Indonesians – all laid out in grid formation and dissected by smooth tarmac roads. There were many Dani in the streets, but only the Indonesians were fully dressed and wearing shoes. Behind the rooftops, as dizzy and fantastic as a Paramount stage set, rose the green-blue slopes of the Snow Mountains.

In the back seat, Akunai was providing one surprise after another.

"You buy this in Jayapura?" asked one of the boys, who had introduced himself as Isaac. He pointed to Akunai's *bilum.*

"No," said Akunai, "my sister made it for me in my village."

"We have these, too," cried Isaac pulling out his own string bag, which was woven a little more closely and with different string. "In Dani word *noken.*"

Akunai took a closer look. "You're right," he said, "it is just like a *bilum.*" He spoke slowly so that Isaac could follow. "Your one is made from bark – from a tree – and mine is made from seisal – from a plant, but in Papua New Guinea we have bark *bilums,* too. Both kinds are made like this," and he rolled an imaginary skein with both his hands into a fine string along his thigh. It was this action, rather than his words, which caused a whoop of recognition from Isaac, who then replayed the tableau to his friends in the back row.

Encouraged by this idea, Akunai pointed to a woven bangle on Isaac's wrist. "We have these in Papua New Guinea, too," he said, "but we wear them here," and he indicated his upper arm. With much deliberation, Isaac removed the bangle and offered it, in both his hands and with an encouraging nod, to Akunai. Respectfully, Akunai slipped the bangle over his elbow and lodged it on his upper arm, Papua New Guinean style.

"My friend," said Niko, touched by the symbolism of the exchange, leaning over to shake his hand again from the front seat. "You tell your family this bracelet from Wamena."

We had emerged on the outskirts of town and the valley opened up before us like one continuous garden. Once we were in the countryside, the tarmac gave way to a chalky white road, as dusty, but a little smoother, than the Simbu Highway. Far away, at the end of the valley, the mountains fused in a haze of blue. There were rice paddies on our right, shimmering emerald green in the bronze light of late afternoon. Above the ripest of these were strings of old cans clinking and flashing against the birds. A couple of Dani tribesmen were walking along the raised bank between the paddies with hoes on their shoulders. On the other side of the road was the familiar sight of *kaukau* mounds, their purple flowers trailing in profusion over the red earth. We were driving, it seemed, along the fine line between Asia and Melanesia.

"Danis eat many, many sweet potatoes, calling them *ipere,*" said Niko.

"We call them *kaukau*," replied Akunai, laughing at the obviousness of his remark. "We eat a lot of them, too."

Everywhere, there were men and women at work, bending over crops, weeding or harvesting, carrying great *noken* full of produce on their backs.

"You certainly work a lot harder than we do," noticed Akunai.

"We work very hard," said Niko. "Only way Dani people get money is sell vegetables to Indonesians in Wamena market."

With a jarring thud, we crossed a great metal suspension bridge over the Baliem River, where women and children were washing. Just as in PNG, there were bush houses here and there by the road, their roofs sprouting flowering vines. Great bushes of lantana shielded beds of marigolds, daisies, buddleia and datura from dust. Occasionally, a pig wandered up onto the road, and chickens, introduced by the Dutch and now living unchallenged by Dani hunting dogs, scratched about for grain.

We arrived at last at Niko's village. Our party poured out of the *bemo* while Akunai and I paid the driver, who briskly turned the bus around and headed straight back for Wamena.

Niko's house was a familiar compromise between bush house and town house. It was square, with wattled walls and tin roof, segregated into compartments by rolls of prefab pitpit. It was set on the road in its own garden, along with a cluster of similar houses. We were met on the path by another group of Niko's *wantoks*, who had heard us arrive. Again, there was the commotion of recognition as Akunai was swamped with hugs and handshakes. By now he was blithely accepting his new status and enjoying the attention. But Niko was eager to get him inside.

"Come with me, my friend, come with me," he urged, tugging at Akunai's arm. "I show you Fafa-Noo-Guinea collection."

Inside, we were ushered to seats at a table strewn with a recent game of cards. Our entourage piled in behind us and leant against the walls or squatted on the floor – wherever they had a good view of Akunai. Occasionally, one would come forward and pat him once again on the shoulder as if he were a talisman for good luck. Someone produced a wad of tobacco and rolled a couple of cigarettes, which were shared around the room.

"Smell this," said Isaac, handing Akunai the wad. "We have good tobacco here from the bush. Not like Indonesian cigarette or Rothman." He spoke scornfully, as if a man is only as strong as the tobacco he smokes. It was native leaf tobacco – *tabak brus* in PNG – and Akunai's refusal to partake of a smoke was clearly a general disappointment. But when he expertly rolled another cigarette from the wad and handed it to one of the boys, the room erupted in whoops of excitement.

Niko had been busy all this while, rifling through a box of papers and knick-knacks that he had slid out from under the table. "Yaah," he announced at last in triumph, producing a heap of greying photocopies with the flourish of a conjurer. He spread them out before Akunai. "Look, we see pictures of you. We know you are like us." He pointed to the smudged and blurry faces smiling out from old magazine articles.

"Last year, tourist show us these pictures of our brothers and we ask to copy on the *masine* in Wamena tourist office."

The only original was a feature on Papua New Guinea from a May 1962 edition of *National Geographic*. The print was almost unreadable in parts and the edges of the page had been softened by hundreds of fingers. Looking over these old images, Niko was as excited as if he were seeing them for the first time.

"See," he said pointing at one. "We know you people also wear penis sheaf. Dani calling it *holim*."

"Well, not all of us do – not any more," said Akunai meekly.

"In my village we used to wear tanget leaves and bark cloths."

But Niko was not discouraged. "Yaah. We have many traditions, too. When missionaries first come to our valley, they try to make us change our cloths. But we don't like white men cloths – they are uncomfortable and dirty, give us bad skin. So missionary say, 'OK. You can wear your *holim*'.

"Then Indonesians come and they say, 'No, you can't wear *holim*'. They start big operation to burn all the *holim* in the valley: 'Operation Koteka' – means 'Operation Penis Sheaf' in Indonesian. But all the time we think of our brothers in Fafa-Noo-Guinea who still free, still can wear their *holim,* and we don't let the Indonesians take them from us. All the time we grow new *holim* in our gardens – they can't stop us. But many people die in battle for our penis sheafs."

As more tea was brewed and more *tabak* smoked, people joined in the conversation, adding their pennysworth, with Isaac or Niko translating. Gradually, as evening drew on, we were told how the Indonesians had burned down villages and tried to move the Dani tribes into tin-roofed shacks. Deprived of the insulating effect of their double-walled bush huts and the companionable warmth of other bodies, many of the older people died. They refused to sleep with blankets and inevitably caught pneumonia.

The Dani's pigs, in particular, had been singled out as being undesirable by the new Muslim masters. The animals were slaughtered in their hundreds or burned alive in their huts. Like the ex-pats in Papua New Guinea, the Indonesians in Irian Jaya thought it was disgusting that the women slept alongside their pigs, or suckled them with their children. But the Indonesians also thought it was filthy to eat them, so their carcasses were left to rot.

Once again, pyres burned in a Highland valley – great piles

of arrows and bows, shields and spears, feathered head-dresses, shells and necklaces, penis gourds and bark skirts – as if a culture could simply evaporate in smoke. Once again, the villagers stored away their most precious belongings, or tried to make some more.

Akunai sat listening with his head bowed, as Niko and Isaac and their friends described their fathers' battles against the enemies of their culture. Occasionally, he shook his head in disgust or sympathy. The battle in Papua New Guinea, it seemed, had not been so clear cut. Repression by the Indonesians had strengthened Dani resolve to maintain their culture. They were impoverished, second-class citizens and they had nothing to lose by preserving their traditional way of life. There were no economic or political opportunities open to them, and the erosive temptations of travel, money and liquor were severely limited by government restrictions. Ironically, under the shadow of Indonesian rule, Dani culture remained protected from the outside world. In PNG, by contrast, the preservation of traditional cultures was inevitably losing out to economic and political priorities; that was the price paid by Papua New Guineans for their higher standard of living and the various freedoms they enjoyed. Preoccupied by the efforts to unite coastal, Highland and island people into one nation, let alone reconcile the warring tribes of the interior provinces or the gangs in the capital, Papua New Guinea hardly cast a glance in the direction of the border. The Melanesians of Irian Jaya, meanwhile, focused on PNG like captives willing on the success of a runaway slave; their spirit lived on through their counterparts across the border.

"Every night we listen to you, our brothers in Fafa-Noo-Guinea," said Niko, "talking to us on our radio. We listen to you on Radio Vanimo. Sometimes you speaking English, sometimes you speaking pidgin, but not many Dani know how to speak pidgin – not many tourist pidgin speaking come to Wamena – no!"

He walked over to the table in the corner where a beaten-up radio took pride of place, a Heath Robinson aerial trailing from it around the wall and out through the window.

"Sounding is best late at night when other radios close down," said Niko, optimistically twiddling a few knobs. "But tonight I think there are storms in the mountains. No radio tonight. Instead we have you my friend – even better!" He patted Akunai affectionately on the shoulder.

"Yaah!" he continued, "Fafa-Noo-Guinea music is excellent music. I have tape," and he brought out a cassette with a picture of five men on the cover in traditional dress holding guitars and *kundu* drums.

"I don't believe it!" Akunai cried. "These are people from near my home town, from Kainantu. These songs are our old tribal songs. Most of them are in Tairox, next-door language to ours, but some are in Kamano. The first track is really a beautiful one."

Niko was thrilled and took back the tape with increased appreciation. "It looks like beautiful music," he said, turning it over in his hands. "One tourist give it to us two years ago but we don't have music *masine* here so we don't know the sound of it yet."

Niko handed the box to Isaac, who wanted to see if the musicians looked anything like Akunai. Every one of them was found to resemble him, much to Akunai's embarrassment; likenesses to members of various clans in the Baliem Valley were also pointed out.

"Look at this fella," said Isaac. "Looks like Thomas from Akima – and this one, look like the son of Wakimo from

Waga-Waga." There were roars of laughter and more congratulatory pats and handshakes.

After some rummaging, a detailed chart was produced and spread across the table. "Show us where you are living," said Isaac. "Point us to where is your home village." Akunai was completely at a loss. I looked over his shoulder and saw that the map was of Asmat, a region to the south of the Baliem Valley, on the coast of Irian Jaya.

"This is not Papua New Guinea," explained Akunai. "This is part of your country. Look." And he found a piece of paper and a pen and began to draw the complete island of New Guinea – the outline of a bird of paradise. Straight through the middle of it he drew the border.

"This half is Irian Jaya," he said, "and this half is Papua New Guinea. And here, in the Highlands, in another valley, is where I live."

Everyone jostled for a closer look, but it was clear from their faces that the sketch meant nothing to them. They had never seen a map of their own valley, let alone the entire island, and the curly scribbles Akunai had drawn to depict the sea meant even less to people who had never seen the real thing.

"Yaah," said Niko, impressed, "this Fafa-Noo-Guinea notebook-and-pen?"

"Yes," laughed Akunai. "They're from a hotel across the border, where we stayed a few weeks ago, in what we call Enga Province. The name is Kaiap Orchid Lodge and it's run by nationals – by people like you and me."

Tears welled up again in Niko's eyes. "My brother," was all he could find to say. How could he explain that Akunai's presence, and all he talked about, surpassed his wildest dreams?

CHAPTER 14

Mumu

Early the next morning, Akunai, Niko and I took a public *bemo* back into Wamena. Niko and his friends were in a state of fresh excitement. They had sent word of our arrival to their chief, who had declared the occasion worthy of a traditional Dani feast, marked by the slaughter of a pig. Preparations were already under way, but the festivities would not begin until late afternoon. We were on our way to the bank and the tobacconist. As guests of honour, it was our duty to supply the whole village with cigarettes. But we also had to pay for the pig. It would cost us two hundred thousand rupiah – almost one hundred American dollars, and a vast sum by Indonesian standards – and there would be an additional stipend to be paid to the chief for distribution in the village.

At first this smacked of profiteering, and I was worried that Niko's hospitality had been a ploy to engage us in lucrative business. Certainly, he had the air of an opportunist. How, otherwise, could he have afforded a radio or the house he had built with his friends – or even his clothes? But there was no doubt that his feelings for Akunai were genuine. He showed him off with the pride of a long-lost brother and could hardly bear to let him out of his sight. At last I concluded that our appreciation of his gesture and the feast itself shouldn't be marred by Niko's desire to earn some money for himself and his village. Pigs were even more precious here than in Papua New Guinea, and we had no right to expect an unconditional gift from people we would probably never see again. We were beyond their system of *payback* and it was highly unlikely that, short of airlifting a pig across the border, we would ever be able to return the favour in kind. We could afford the charge – Niko knew that. He treated it as a straightforward transaction of goodwill, and we, I felt, should do the same.

Akunai was not quite sure. But, lulled by the beauty of the morning and Niko's persistence, he felt neither willing nor able to express his doubts. I was looking forward to the prospect of spending a night in a Dani village; Akunai, I felt, could not quite rid himself of his innate fear of strange tribes.

All the shops in Wamena town were clustered within a single compound behind the *bemo* stop on the main street. At the entrance, an Indonesian meat seller was hacking at the ragged carcass of a cow. The carcass was buzzing with flies as noisy and persistent as the crowd around it, and only the Indonesians were buying meat. The Dani, mostly men, hung back and watched, holding hands or hugging their bare chests in the chill morning air. Some of them had feathers in their hair, like Engans, or sprigs of fern or daisies, or little knitted *noken*, or hats, of cuscus fur. Their chests were hung with shells, seeds or some other talisman to ward off evil spirits that might snatch a man's soul from his sternum. Their penis gourds doubled as a wallet, with a few precious rupiah notes stuffed down the open end. It would take a pickpocket with nerve to rip off a Dani warrior.

Many of the Indonesians, by contrast, wore medallions around their necks, and shirts from the 1970s with pointed collars and stylised prints. They sported plastic mining hats or motorbike helmets like London businessmen wearing bowlers – as a mark of caste as much as fashion. They threw their weight about in the general throng and the Dani instinctively made way for them.

Inside, the market was charged with noise, a cloud of continuous chatter picked out by the staccato interruptions of dogs yelping, pigs squealing, children shouting and babies crying. The perimeter stalls were the exclusive province of Indonesian traders. There were children's toys on sale – blow-up Batman figures and lime-green furry trolls – as well as jars of candy, colouring books and plastic beads; there were spice stalls and flour stalls; food stalls with fish cakes and rice balls, tinned food and instant noodles; washing powder and soap stalls; cotton and cloth; ballpoint pens and exercise books. And at the front of each little Aladdin's cave prowled the storekeeper, one eye out for customers, the other on the cash box.

The central floor space, however, was the arena of the Dani farmers. It was exploding with the bounty of the valley, with fruit and vegetables bigger and better than anything Europe or America or Asia could have offered. There were bunches of carrots as big as small cucumbers, and yellow and green cucumbers as big as small marrows. There were baskets of peanuts, and branches bristling with bananas and plantains. There were mountains of sweet potatoes – almost a dozen different kinds – and taros and yams; there were tomatoes and red onions, ginger and chillies, soya and rice, pineapples and oranges, coffee beans and tea leaves, and home-grown Highland honey.

Akunai could hardly believe his eyes. "They must be making

a fortune," he said. "Look at this stuff – it's better quality than the food we import from Australia. This is what we should be doing in Papua New Guinea – we're Highlanders, we're farmers, we have the same soil, we can produce the best food in the world."

"Yaah," said Niko, who had taken to greeting all of Akunai's comments with the same response, "but this is very cheap food, grow everywhere in the valley. We must sell many vegetables for one bar of soap. Not possible to become a rich man selling this kind of vegetables."

It was the only way, though, that the Dani could get cash for clothes, sugar, soap, medicine or *bemo* rides, and so they produced vegetables in great quantities, much of which went to waste. Very little produce ever left the valley. Even Jayapura was supplied with vegetables and fruit from Java.

"Why can't you export it?" asked Akunai. "Send it to other places in the country, to the coast. They would pay a big price for food like this."

Niko looked blank, but appreciative. "Yaah. Thank you very *mux*, my friend." The idea, but not the intention, was lost on him.

It was galling for Akunai to see such obvious inequality of labour. The Dani were still living in the *taim bilong masta*. But at the same time, he knew the situation in Papua New Guinea was perhaps more insidious. Where the way was open for his own people to make a substantial success of commercial agriculture, they had neither the enterprise nor the unity that the Dani had found under the constraints of Indonesian rule.

At the back of the market I found a stall with wooden bowls full of potash. "Dani use this salt for our food," said Niko. "We fill bamboos with water from local brine pool and cook them on the fire. Water disappear and this salt comes out from bamboo."

It tasted as dry as dust with a faint tinge of woodsmoke. "This is what the Highland people in Papua New Guinea used to make," said Akunai, "before we could buy salt from the coast."

As we were leaving the market I spotted some canisters of table salt at the back of an Indonesian food stall, and dived in on impulse to buy them. I hoped they would be a fitting personal contribution for a guest at a pig feast. But the salt might also, I thought selfishly, render the food more palatable. Memories of *mumus* in Akunai's village were already spoiling my appetite.

At midday we set off for the village, loaded up with salt, cigarettes and thousands of rupiah. We walked half a mile down the main road and then turned up a narrow track towards the mountains. Taro gardens flourished on either side of the path, their huge heart-shaped leaves nodding in the breeze. There were paddocks of *kunai* grass and a small potato field, freshly harvested. Several pigs had been let loose in the field to rootle about in the earth for leftover tubers; they snortled with pleasure, unaware of the task they were performing in ploughing the soil for the next crop. Their minders, two women in hooped string skirts with *bilums* on their backs, stood up to watch us go by.

After a while, we passed into a grove of trees and crossed a substantial, fast-flowing stream. From the depths of the wood a cry went up, and Niko pointed to a watchtower, well disguised among the trees, and a *wasman* scampering down the ladder to run off with the news. A hundred yards further on, we came upon the perimeter fence and the entrance to the village. By now, Akunai was looking extremely anxious.

We were met by the elders of the village, who were waiting by the men's house, or *honai*, at the far end of the compound.

They were armed with bows and arrows and ceremonial spears. All of them wore penis gourds, some with the tuft of a cuscus tail bristling out of the top. The chief came forward with a bare-toothed grin of welcome. One of his legs was stiff and straight, and dragged as he walked; but his body was fit and powerful, and glistened with an insulating layer of pig fat. His eyes were thickly outlined with charcoal, which gave him a menacing but not unattractive glare of authority. He extended his hand in greeting and let out an unexpected *'wa-wa-wa-wa-wa'* like the excited cry of a bird.

"This is our chief," said Niko, "name Pasam Faluk. He say you welcome."

Chief Faluk spoke neither English nor Indonesian, but his bearing had a dignity that transcended language. Beside this eagle, Niko was a squawking jackdaw. He was greeted with the same enthusiastic *'wa-wa-wa-wa-wa',* but I got the impression that the villagers treated him with caution, perhaps a little disdain. He had crossed over into another world and, though instrumental as a go-between, no longer belonged exclusively to the village. He was as ingratiating among his own people as he was with us.

Gingerly, I offered the chief a cigarette. He nodded approvingly and put it behind his ear like a workman on a building site. Emboldened by this success, I pulled the salt canisters out of my bag and handed them over. I was surprised by the chief's immediate comprehension of what they were. He adeptly shook a little salt into his hand to taste it, just to make sure; then his face broke into a broad, all-encompassing grin. He passed the canisters on to the elders and came forward to grasp my hand in thanks.

With this gesture, the elders relaxed noticeably. They came

forward to receive cigarettes from Niko, and the tension of the meeting dissolved in comfortable puffs of smoke. Niko introduced Akunai as a brother from Papua New Guinea, and the old men patted his legs and flicked their penis gourds in appreciation.

Soon the compound began to fill with women and children, who ventured out from the safety of their houses or from behind the perimeter fence. Several of the younger warriors emerged from the men's house as if gracing a society ball with an appearance. They wore their penis gourds and cockerel feathers with a jauntiness designed to turn the heads of the women. Akunai was rattled by their presence and flinched defensively – just as he had done as a little boy when armed warriors had appeared on one of his father's crusades. But these were not tribal enemies, distrustful of outsiders; these men were his hosts, on home ground and used to the presence of strangers. Though this village was not on the tourist map as such, it was still close enough to Wamena to encounter the occasional trekker; and sometimes Niko would interest a visitor in sponsoring a traditional feast, like the one we were about to witness.

"Chief Faluk say you come sit here," said Niko pointing to a seat in the shade. "He say thank you very *mux* my friends for come to his village. He say you tell your family, your friends in Fafa-Noo-Guinea, that you have big welcome at house of Chief Faluk."

After the excitement of our arrival, the village resumed its easy calm. The children, quickly accustomed to our presence, scattered in search of more amusing distractions. A couple of pigs, one built like a tank, wandered about the compound, rubbing their backs against the corner posts. A woman sitting in her doorway making a *noken* stretched out her hand to scratch the biggest pig as it wandered by; it halted in its tracks and grunted appreciatively. The woman's fingers had all been amputated at the knuckle.

"This old Dani tradition," Niko explained. "When children die or husband, father, mother, woman has one finger cut. Like this." He demonstrated how a tourniquet would be applied on the upper arm to numb the sensation in the hand; then a man, perhaps the woman's brother, would chop off the outstretched finger with an axe. Some sort of compress would be applied to the wound to stem the flow of blood.

"Sometimes women cut all their fingers," said Niko, "if many of her family die. But always keep the fingers up to here," (and he pointed to the knuckle), "and both thumbs so they can do their gardening."

Akunai was familiar with the practice. "You can still see some of the very old women around Kainantu with missing fingers. But here the women are much younger."

"Not many women still cut their fingers," agreed Niko. "Christian religion says it is bad custom. But some Dani women like to show sorrow for their dead ones, like to tell the spirits they are sorry."

I was reminded of pitiful necklaces I had seen in Goroka's museum – bamboo chains threaded with the mummified fingers of loved ones that had been worn by the Anga people in the Wanemara district well into the 1950s and '60s. One necklace had moved me to tears. It displayed, amongst dangling chains of pitpit, the tiny, clenched fists of a baby and the longer, skeletal hand of the wearer's husband. It was a macabre, yet strangely touching, gesture to the dead. The amputation of living fingers was a similar exercise; for all its savagery, it was a measure of self-sacrifice and remembrance that helped the bereaved come to terms with their loss. For a warrior people, it was certainly more demonstrative than the empty reassurances of Christianity.

"Some women," said Akunai, "used to say they could feel their missing fingers, as if they were still there. It was like being reminded that the spirits of the dead are still with us, just as they were in life, even though we can't see them."

Eventually, the stones for the oven were red-hot, the taros and sweet potatoes had been brought in from the gardens, and enough leaves and grass had been scythed to insulate the cooking mound. Now was the time to kill the pig. I cannot say I had been looking forward to this moment. But the proceedings were even messier than I had imagined. It was traditional for the animal to be killed with a single arrow shot through the heart. At first I was enthusiastic about the humanity of this method – no stressful blood wagons here, no haphazard electric stunners, no hooks or meat cleavers, just one clean, instantaneous blow delivered by a friend. But I had not anticipated the time it would take to catch the animal. Despite my concern, I found myself stifling a laugh as Dani warriors, their penis gourds waggling, slipped and slithered around the compound after their pig. By the time the animal was cornered, it was sweating profusely and pumping more adrenalin through its body than would ever have passed quality control at Sainsbury's.

Squealing horrendously, it was carried by two warriors into the middle of the yard. Its wiry, black hair bristled in alarm. Slowly and deliberately the marksman came forward to within about ten feet of his target. The pig bucked madly against his captors, anticipating the shot, as the arrow left the bow and struck him deep in the chest. But that was not the end of the matter. I had expected death throes, perhaps a gasp or two, but no more. Instead, when the animal was lowered to the ground and released, it got up and began to pelt around the yard, screaming. After a while, it slowed down a little and wandered around dazed, crashing into fences and posts, still steady on its feet despite the arrow in its chest. At last even the Dani began to feel an extra hand would be necessary.

It was taboo to inflict a further wound on the animal, so the warriors were restricted to making sure the first arrow did its job. They caught the pig again and then, with a couple of men holding it down, the marksman stabbed the arrow further into the wound. Still the pig snorted and bucked, though it frothed a little now at the mouth. When it was released, it looked as if it might revive again, so the men began to press their feet against the base of the arrow, stamping the life out of its heart.

"Good, strong pig," said Niko proudly. The children, who had watched the proceedings with glee from the top of the fence, clambered down to examine the body like self-appointed coroners and pronounced the animal dead. The village dogs came forward too, to sniff the animal and lick the blood from its orifices and the stains on the ground. A small fire was lit in the square and the pig was turned over the flames to burn off the bristles. The carcass blew into a balloon until it was nothing more than a charred, bloated effigy of itself. It was laid on a bed of banana leaves, sliced nose to tail with a razor-sharp sliver of bamboo and laid out in one flat piece like a skin with the meat still on. Dogs dragged the entrails off to eat in peace.

Chief Faluk was pleased. "He say his pig die well," said Niko. "Now his guests will eat well, too."

We adjourned to watch the less harrowing task of making the oven, though I was so shaken that I could hardly move. The stones were taken one by one from the fire with long staves split at one end to act like giant tweezers, and dropped into a shallow nest of leaves. Wet grass was laid over the stones, and on top of all this went the pig, wrapped in a wadding of leaves to preserve the juices. Purple sweet potatoes were packed together over the pig and dressed in more leaves. Finally, the whole mound was wrapped in grass and tied with string into a neat, steamy parcel. It was very similar to the earth ovens in PNG, except that there the food was baked in a pit and covered with earth, with water funnelled in to help steam the potatoes.

Over the next two hours, the grass oven changed from a luminous green to dank, dark brown. There was a smell of stewing vegetation not unlike the aroma of school cabbage. At last, the steaming parcel was unwrapped, the scalding leaves were tossed aside and the sweet potatoes were flung out, thudding onto the ground to cool. Finally, the pig was lifted out, wrapped in a slimy cocoon of banana leaves and presided over by men who swatted away inquisitive dogs, flies and children.

The afternoon was fading fast, and the skies were now full of threatening storm clouds. A flicker of lightning spat out a warning strike at the mountain tops above us. But there was no way to curtail the ritual. First, each piece of pork was carefully laid aside to be handed out to each family by Chief Faluk. Then the potatoes were distributed by the women, as the first raindrops began to fall, slapping on banana leaves. Soon the thatch was rustling from the impact of the heavy shower and the party scattered for shelter with their arms full of hot potatoes.

Akunai and I were shown by Niko to the visitors' house – a small, round thatched hut with old hay on the floor and a raised wooden platform which served as a bed. Niko and I sat on the edge of the platform and Akunai settled himself on the floor with his back against the wattle as if it were his own hut at home. Niko lit the wick in a small jar of paraffin on a tea box.

"We stay in here," said Niko. "Chief Faluk will bring us our food. It is his wife's pig, so he must take it to each house. He will take it to the *big men's* houses first."

So we sat in the fading light, listening to the rain on the thatch and picking at soft, chestnutty potatoes. Occasionally, we saw Chief Faluk limp past through the puddles on his errand. Our portion was delivered halfway down the line. A whole leg, because we were honoured guests, was laid ceremoniously on a banana leaf on the floor.

"*Wa-wa-wa-wa-wa,*" said Niko by way of thanks, as the chief withdrew. He pulled off a large chunk of fat – the 'best' bit – and handed it to me. It was cold by now and slimy from its travels in the rain, and at that moment seemed even less appetising than a live sago grub. I tried to think of other things as I warmed it in my cheek; it tasted of smoke and boiled cabbage, with a sweaty aftertaste. The skin to which the fat was still attached was rubbery and impenetrable. There was no question of swallowing it whole. Surreptitiously, aided by the darkness in the hut, I coughed it into my hand and slid it down the sleeve of my sweatshirt.

Niko offered me another piece. I refused. He insisted. I said I was full. He told me to save it for later. I put it next to me on the platform and waited for a chance to go out and bury it – or better still to pass it to Akunai who was licking his fingers on his third piece.

As the rain abated, and darkness closed in, Chief Faluk came back to our hut, dragging his leg stiffly. He sat down with his leg stretched out in front. He was clearly exhausted.

"Chief leg no good," explained Niko, like an actor giving an aside, "he break it many years ago." The chief smiled broadly, his lips drawing back over even, white teeth. His eyeliner had run slightly in the rain but he looked as dignified as ever. He spoke aloud into the middle of the room.

"Chief say his pig is good?" translated Niko.

I told him it was delicious and offered him my spare piece.

"No," said Niko firmly, "it very shame for man to eat from his wife's pig. Chief must eat only *ipere* – sweet potato – tonight."

Chief Faluk ate his sweet potato in the light from the candle, cockerel feathers nodding and penis gourd wagging against his chest. He could have come from any point in time over the past ten thousand years.

At last, the ceremony of food was over and the chief pronounced himself satisfied. He then pulled something from the tip of his penis gourd.

"Chief say he want you tell your mother, your father, you made traditional feast with Dani. Something you remember this day, this one good pig feast."

The chief leant forward and motioned for me to hold out my hand. What he put in it felt at first like some sort of bracelet but the ends were not tied together. It was rubbery and hairy at the same time, with a kind of tassel at one end. I held it up to the light for a better look. It took several seconds to realise I was holding the pig's tail. The chief beamed his entrancing smile.

"Thank you," I managed to say, returning his smile. "I am deeply honoured," and I genuinely was. The chief flicked his penis gourd with approval.

"He say you must put the tail in your bag," said Niko, "so the mouse doesn't run away with it."

I tucked it away in the top pocket of my rucksack, and there it remained, forgotten, for the next two weeks until a customs official checked my bag in Australia and found it putrefying in a mould of wet paper.

There was a knock at our door and in came Samuel, another friend of Niko's, and his brother Akulek. They shook hands with the chief and then with us, and took their place on the floor of the hut.

"These my friends say want to hear story about Fafa-Noo-Guinea. They have brother, member of OPM, who is catched by Fafa-Noo-Guinea police over the border."

Samuel and Akulek had not been at the feast, but had walked all day to get to the village when they heard we were here. They wanted to give us a letter for their brother, from whom they had not heard for five years. Occasionally, they learnt through the grapevine, via tribal men who had crossed the border and returned, that Namelek was still alive. The latest information was that he had been detained in the Blackwater Refugee Camp near Vanimo, where many other Dani tribesmen were held. It was Samuel who did all the talking; his brother Akulek sat silently, watching Akunai with wild, excited eyes.

"Samuel say his brother disappeared in big battle of 1977," said Niko, "when Indonesians come to Wamena and kill many Dani. Many villages burned down and many of our people – young men – try to escape to Fafa-Noo-Guinea. He say you bring him long lost brother one letter. He say thank you very, very *mux*."

Samuel's letter was composed in English with the help of the Catholic Mission and painstakingly printed in capitals; the words hovered neatly above the lines. Every 'i' was dotted with a perfect circle, and there was not a single blot of ink or crossing out.

25-7-91

Dear my old brother,

Greetings in love of jesus Christ.

I am from Samuel give you "HALLO" for Namelek, Bertina and Agustinus in Black Water Camp (Vanimo).

Your fathers two men had die called:

1. Kunambiri Walesi in 1979
2. Uakpaga Walesi in 1989
3. Wandelewe Kiangga in 1989

So the ones who lives here only the children of them and the condition of us are well because god allways accompany and protect us where we live. And we allways eat some sweet potatoes everyday because our basic food in Dani. And we sleep in Honai every night. So what food do you allways eat everyday? I think you have some good foods in PNG.

One day it was a bright day and it was a good weather we allways sad and remembered for you.

The one who is sending this letter the youngest boy of Kunambiri and this is your young brother called Samuel Walesi so I have been studying english for three years and I can speak english well. I wish will come with you, nowadays I have been guide in Wamena. If you want to reply my letter, you may send it through someone from PNG want to visit in Indonesia (Irian Jaya) you may send it so that I will easy to get it.

How are you? I hope you are well and happy because god be with you.

My love friend Namelek I hope to see you again the next times so that we live together in PNG.

I hope you may give me your address and some photos to hold.
Thanks!

Yours sincerely,
Samuel Walesi

We agreed to deliver the letter and Niko handed out a celebratory round of cigarettes. The chief took a long, luxurious drag through clenched teeth and addressed Akunai.

"Chief Faluk say you, how many Indonesians do you have in Fafa-Noo-Guinea?" asked Niko.

Akunai smiled. "We have none. Maybe one or two at the embassy in Moresby, but I've never seen one."

"Thank you very *mux*," said Niko, thrilled, "I tell the chief."

Chief Faluk flicked his gourd and laughed when he heard the translation. "He say you very lucky. He say you are one true brother."

"Tell him we have our own government," said Akunai, "with our own president, a blackfella like us."

Niko looked stunned. Akunai had told Niko this before and I thought he had understood, but clearly the idea was still inconceivable. When the chief heard, he, too, looked perplexed.

"See," said Akunai, reaching into his pocket and withdrawing a fifty kina note. "This is Michael Somare – our first prime minister in Papua New Guinea parliament in 1975." He handed around the note. The chief beamed down upon it, took out an Indonesian rupiah from his penis gourd and compared the two notes, laughing at the difference.

"And this one, here," said Akunai, "this is a two kina note and this is ten kina. They have all the symbols of old currency on it. There's kina and toea shells, dogs' teeth and pigs' tusks, and stone axes and feathers, and this one has *kundu* drums and shield on it."

"Yes, yes," cried Niko, "these are all our old monies."

"And this is our national symbol," said Akunai, turning the notes over, "the bird of paradise. We put it on our stamps and our flag and our Air Niugini airplanes. And this," he said capping it all with a flourish, "is our twenty kina note." A boar's head was engraved across it, bristling with hair and long white tusks, its lips drawn back in a snarl to reveal its teeth.

The chief responded with a *'wa-wa-wa-wa-wa'*, his face creasing into a great grin of pleasure. It was the ultimate proof that Papua New Guinea was in charge of its own destiny. Somewhere, at last, the pig was rightfully honoured. It had official status in Papua New Guinea.

"Will you tell the chief he can keep it," said Akunai to Niko, and he handed the boar's head to Chief Faluk. The remaining notes were shared out between the others.

Eventually, the chief yawned, exhausted by his role as host, and muttered something to Niko. "You come now, sleep in men's house," said Niko to Akunai. "You are one Dani brother. Your friend, she sleep here in visitors' house, having comfortable bed here."

Akunai looked more than apprehensive, but there was no avoiding the honour. Picking up his bag, he left the hut after the others, with a bleak "See you in the morning, then." I watched them march across the compound towards the great domed *honai*, before extinguishing the candle and lying down to sleep.

It was a night I hope never to repeat. The platform was solid hardwood and made the springy pitpit bed in Akunai's house seem like goosedown; only with all my clothes underneath me was there any hope of sleep. Then the scratching began. As I hung suspended in a waking dream, the walls came alive with scuttling vermin. They rustled through the thatch, scurried over the floor, knocked over the candle, tiptoed across my bed. I had forgotten to get rid of the piece of fat I'd left by my bedside, and the hut was under siege from rats. No sooner had I grown accustomed to their gymnastics than my clothes seemed to be biting me. When I turned on my torch I saw nothing, but I soon realised that the entire contents of my rucksack and bed were infested with fleas.

At dawn, I finally sank into an exhausted sleep. I was woken only an hour or two later by Akunai, who looked more dishevelled and battered than I imagined I looked myself.

"Gee, it's a relief to get out of there," he said, climbing in through the door and sitting back against the wall like a long-distance runner who has just passed the finishing line. "I never thought I'd make it to another day. I couldn't sleep all night. It was terrifying in that men's house. There must have been ten people all snoring away and grinding their teeth, and their penis gourds were hitting the floor every time they turned over."

He mopped his brow with his sleeve.

"I got really scared in the middle of the night when everyone else was asleep. We have legends in my village that your spirit leaves you when you are asleep and wanders about the countryside. And suddenly I thought I was lying amongst dead men.

"Then this rat landed on my leg and I kicked out and woke the man next to me. Then I noticed Niko had gone. He was sleeping beside me one minute, and the next he had disappeared like magic and I thought I might vanish as well. I kept listening for every sound, but all I could hear were rats and mosquitoes. I just wanted to hear normal noises – like a cock crowing or some birds. It seemed like dawn was never going to happen."

He was laughing now at the demons of the night, but even so he seemed unnerved. Despite the hospitality of the Dani and the warmth they showed their Papua New Guinean brother, Akunai could not rid himself of his inborn distrust of other tribes. The Dani stories of persecution and the more nebulous terrors of the spirit world had fuelled his unease. The border was only one hundred and sixty miles away, but in logistical terms, Papua New Guinea might as well have been on the other side of the world.

By the time we were ready to return to Wamena, most of the villagers had assembled outside. Akunai and I went up to the *honai* to say goodbye to the elders and Chief Faluk. Although the charcoal around the chief's eyes had faded overnight and he wore no head-dress, he still cut an awesome figure. He pressed a gift into my hand. It was his own string of mouth harps – two of them blackened with woodsmoke and seasoned by a thousand long evenings, a third cut from fresh bamboo. The PNG equivalents were called *nonto* and were much larger; the chief's harps were tiny, delicate instruments, wafer thin and strung together with the finest woven thread. He held me by the hand and looked deep into my eyes, impressing the gift upon me. On the brink of tears, I held his gaze in response as long as I could.

When we left the village, there was a chorus of applause from flicking penis gourds and a round of *'wa-wa-wa-wa-wa'*. We stopped a *bemo* and settled in our seats, and I took one last look back towards the village. The chief had come to see us off and was waving in a circular motion, away from his body and then back towards his chest, as if signalling that we should one day return.

A couple of days later, Niko, Isaac and their friends assembled to see us off at the airport. They stood amongst the puddles on the tarmac, excited by the notion that we were off to PNG, but dejected at the thought of our departure.

"You come back 1994, '95, '96 perhaps?" asked Niko, clinging to Akunai's arm with last-ditch enthusiasm. "Bringing pop group from P-and-G, Fafa-Noo-Guinea my friend."

"Why not next year," said Akunai on the spur of the moment, "1992?"

"Yaaaah," cried Niko, his eyes popping with pleasure.

"Good, I very, very happy. My brother. You give us greetings to your prime minister. You say he doing one good job for our people in P-and-G."

Chapter 15

Hailans Kalsarel So

Akunai was overjoyed to be back amongst Papua New Guineans. Vanimo was the antithesis of all that was Indonesian – it was calm, peaceful and unambitious. It instantly restored his faith in the ethnic identity of his country. Towards the end of our stay in the Baliem Valley, he had become anxious about the effect of new trade links with Irian Jaya. There was a road already under construction between Jayapura and Vanimo – the first ever to cross the border – and commercial dialogue between the two countries had begun to thaw the frostiness of political relations. Akunai was worried that closer exchanges would damage PNG's traditional culture.

"You've seen what these Indonesians are like," he had said, as we sat out our last evening in Irian Jaya. "They'll start fishing out our waters like the Japanese, and tearing down our forests, and seducing us with a load of cheap, plastic rubbish. How are we going to resist this kind of a cultural landslide?"

At the time, his forebodings had conjured up images of Highland children succumbing to Teenage Mutant Ninja Turtle mania; of warriors wearing plastic flowers in their hair; of village women carrying plastic handbags and wearing plastic shoes. Where the Dani had been protected because of their poverty, the Papua New Guineans, he believed, might abuse their spending power on a new ersatz materialism, instead of on *sing-sings*, pig feasts and beer.

But now that we were back on home ground, these fears fell into perspective. We were walking along the coastal road, amongst frangipani trees which dropped their flowers of white, pink and yellow on the sweaty tarmac. People were fishing from the quayside and splashing in the water, or just sitting on the beach watching the sea. Life in PNG was a matter of the moment, drifting from one day to the next. The same reluctance to compete in business that had crushed Akunai's efforts to start a national coffee company would in part guard the country against the more insidious aspects of trade with Indonesia. Accruing wealth, whether financial or material, was simply not part of the national culture. It would take more than a trade agreement to change that.

There were only two days left of what Akunai called our 'trip of a lifetime'. There seemed no better way to spend the time than by attending the country's biggest *sing-sing*, the colourful and competitive Highlands Cultural Show – or Hailans Kalsarel So – to be held in Mt Hagen. But we had one last task to perform before leaving Vanimo, and we threw ourselves into it with determination.

We had been surprised to learn that the Blackwater Camp for refugees from Irian Jaya had been transferred from Vanimo for security reasons to somewhere near Kiunga, deep in the swamp-lands of Western Province. But as luck would have it, we had returned to PNG on a Saturday and a series of local rugby matches was in progress in the middle of town. If there were any

Dani people left in Vanimo – and we had been led to believe that some had avoided transfer to Kiunga by attaching themselves to the local missions – we would find them at the rugby.

Getting in contact with them, however, proved to be as tricky as a cold-war assignation in Gorky Park. The approaches we made to groups of spectators sitting under fig trees were met with black looks and evasive shrugs. No one seemed willing to talk. At last, as we were ready to give up, a small, stocky man in a brightly coloured *bilum* hat caught up with us. He was nervous and self-conscious but we persuaded him to follow us to our hotel where we could talk in private.

Over a number of SPs, which gradually increased his confidence, he began to open up. His friends at the rugby match had advised him not to talk to us, but when he heard us mention Namelek Walesi, he had to know if we had news of his family. Namelek was a good friend of his, they were from the same village in the Baliem Valley, and he knew how much Namelek missed his family. They had gone on hunting expeditions together as kids and he remembered Namelek's younger brother, Samuel, who had given us the letter.

After being captured in PNG, Namelek had found work with the Baptists who looked after the refugee camp. When the camp moved, the church went with it and Namelek and a few others from the mission joined some freedom fighters in the OPM and fled to the bush. They were still in the vicinity of Vanimo and this man could get the letter to Namelek via a contact in the Movement.

We were reluctant to hand over the letter straight away, so we probed a little further to see if this 'West Irian' could be trusted. As he told his story, reinforced with impressive detail and corroborating descriptions of life in his home village, our suspicions were allayed. He could be none other than a bona fide Dani. Later, he even played my little Dani harp to prove it.

But his story was a harrowing one. Namelek and he had left the Baliem Valley during intense fighting against the Indonesians in 1977. The Dani spears were no match for heli-copter gun ships and heavy artillery, and many young warriors had fled towards the safety of the border in an effort to secure some weapons from the outside world. They had hoped to join forces with other factions in the resistance. Our storyteller was seventeen then, and full of anger and energy. But he and his fellow villagers hadn't bargained on the nature of the terrain lying between them and the border. It took a full month to reach PNG, by which time some of them had died of malaria. They lived off wild pigs, cassowaries and birds' eggs. When they finally reached the Hindenberg River, it was the largest body of water they had ever seen. They had to build a raft and float downstream; one of the men drowned.

After the full moon, they reached the Bewani Mountains. But the Papua New Guinean border patrols, tipped off by the Indonesians, were waiting for them. The police were not hard on the refugees. They disliked the Indonesians as much as the Dani did, and would often let their prisoners escape; theirs was only a political task, after all. They had to take a certain number of refugees back to the Indonesians to show that they were doing their job, but most of the Dani in this man's group wound up in the Blackwater Camp.

At first they were happy just to be living in a free country. Life in the camp wasn't too bad and inmates were allowed to visit town one day a week. They learned pidgin quickly and some even got jobs. But our friend began to miss his family, and worried about how they would cope without him. He decided to escape and walk back to the Baliem Valley. But just a few days after he'd managed to get back across the border, he was recaptured, this time by the Indonesian army. He was taken to jail in Jayapura and beaten senseless. After several hard beatings over a period of three weeks, he managed to escape again and found his way back to PNG.

In 1985 he tried again. This time he made it across the mountains and the great Hindenberg River, all the way back to his village. But he was greeted with tragic news: the Indonesians had burnt down his village and killed every member of his family in retaliation for his escape from prison in Jayapura. As he reached the end of his story, he was on the verge of tears.

"I take messages for the OPM," he said at last, "but I will not fight any more. I am too tired. I have lost all my family. The only thing I have left is my freedom. This I have earned from staying in PNG for eight years. I don't want to lose that. I will never go back."

A faint suggestion of chanting rose and fell on the wind. The rugby crowds were breaking up. The West Irian – we still did not know his name – folded Samuel's letter into the waistband of his trousers and slipped quietly away.

The mountains around Mt Hagen had never looked so beautiful as Akunai and I flew towards them for the last time. Remnants of early-morning mist fluttered around the peaks in tattered flags. The shadows were still deep and dark in the ravines.

"I feel like Busybee," said Akunai, "coming back to Goroka after spending all that time in Enga and Mendi. Except I've been to places he could never even dream of. I wonder what he would think of those people and all that noise in Jayapura. Whatever our problems, we've got a good life here. I never knew we were so lucky."

The sun began to glow on the ridges, warming the villages which perched on top like rows of straw hats. Soon we were flying up the Hagen Valley, with mountains sheer on either side and little garden plots bright beneath us. The bottle-green grids of coffee and tea plantations stretched out across the valley floor.

"I never thought I'd be so happy to see them," said Akunai. "Do you remember driving through all those plantations on our way to Wabag? Seems like a hundred years ago."

And so it did. But as I watched Akunai looking out of the airplane window, I realised I had little more idea of what he was thinking than when we first started out together.

"Do you feel it's been worth it?" I ventured to ask. "Going to Porgera and Lake Kutubu and Irian Jaya?"

He looked back out of the window. "It's probably changed my life," he said flatly. But he gave no indication of whether this was a good or a bad thing.

When our wheels touched down on the Hagen airstrip, our fellow passengers sent up a cheer like an away team arriving at their match. Though this was a strictly Highlands Show, representatives from the islands and the coast could not resist making an appearance. There were shields and drums in the hold, and canisters containing feathers in the luggage racks. Bows and arrows and spears, even of a ceremonial nature, had been banned from the event; they proved too much of a temptation for warriors bent on asserting their machismo. There were risks enough involved in bringing traditional enemies together without the provocation of ready-made weapons. Somehow, though, weapons managed to be slipped through the net. The tribesmen's *banaras* and *spias* were as much a part of their finery, their *bilas*, as anything else, and they would defy a government ban for the sake of ceremony.

By way of preparation, while we were waiting for our luggage, Akunai told me how to react if I was tear-gassed. "Just cover your nose and mouth with your shirt or something, so you don't breathe too much in," he said encouragingly. "And whatever you do, don't wipe your eyes. It makes them sting far more than if you just let your tears get rid of it. Oh, and always run in the direction of the crowd."

Last year, a group from the Wahgi Valley had instigated a riot when they had failed to win the trophy for best turned-out tribe twice in a row. They had arrived at the show dressed exactly as they had been the year before when they had won – so why, they reasoned, had they not won it again? There were also chilling tales of poisoning and shoot-outs at the last show, which had been held in Goroka. So fierce was the competition that someone had tried to slip a lethal dose of malaria tablets into one of the judge's food, and several other judges received death threats before the results were issued.

"Nowadays," said Akunai, "it's really difficult to find anyone brave or stupid enough to judge the Highland Show. Some people do it for the money – there can be a lot of bribery involved – but even so, they have to live under armed guard until everyone has gone home again."

Apparently, there was always a riot when the winner was announced. "That's when we really have to be careful. Try to get back to our hotel before that happens. Otherwise, it's every person for themselves and hell breaks loose."

"It sounds like we'll need Busybee and his *busnaip*."

"Yeah," said Akunai laughing. "He'll be sorry to have missed this. You remember when we got stuck in that *sing-sing* in the middle of the road to Porgera? I can still see him sitting on top of the truck surrounded by all those wild, crazy Engans. Jeez, he looked scared."

There was an atmosphere of carnival in the airport compound. Hagen airstrip was a good six miles from town and the yard was packed with people competing for a lift. There were late participants, ex-pats up from Moresby and even the odd private plane that had flown in from Australia. And there were tourists by the busload, clinging to their groups like startled sheep.

It was disorientating to see so many *waitman*. For most of my trip with Akunai, the only white face I'd seen had been the one that surprised me in a mirror. My eyes had grown accustomed to expecting one or two whites at most, in any crowd; this new ratio had me reeling. The tourists seemed to make themselves doubly conspicuous with defenceless skin and sun-dazzled eyes, peeling noses and mosquito-bitten legs – and screeching voices. En masse, the Caucasian race was a discordant rabble, an amazing cacophony of shrieks and squeaks and barks and yelps. Akunai seemed to rise above it – or maybe I was only just beginning to notice his chameleon-like ability. He seemed to adapt to the rowdiness of the *waitman* far more easily than I could.

The show attracted tour groups from Australia, Japan and, above all, the States, with special flights laid on direct from Miami to Mt Hagen. The brochures at reception in our hotel advertised 'The Noble Savage in his Native Environment', as though announcing a visit to a theme park: 'Return to the Stone Age'; 'Come face to face with fiercesome tribal warriors'; 'Visit Pre-history'.

When the time came for the hotel minibus to depart for the show, I was squeezed in between life-sized replicas of the Flintstones. On one side of me was Barney Rubble, whose stomach was doing battle with the waistband of his shorts; his friend, on the other side, wore a Simpsons T-shirt, and talked across me, his hairy arm lying along the back of my seat.

It came as a shock to hear these people talk about Papua New Guineans as if they were a species in the zoo. Akunai, in his freshly pressed shorts and Lacoste T-shirt, clearly did not count. He sat at the front of the minibus looking disinterestedly out of the window.

"Look, Earl," said Wilma Flintstone, pointing out of the window, "that man's almost naked. Do you think those are real leaves he's wearing in his skirt?"

"Don't look, honey," her husband guffawed, "anything you see there ain't gonna be comparable to what you can get at home."

"Will the people at the *sing-sing* let us take pictures?" Wilma asked the driver. "They won't be worried that we'll be taking away their spirits?"

"No," said the driver, calmly. "They will be taking photos, too."

———

The showground was swarming with people. Above the heads of the crowd was a sea of fluttering feathers, and an eerie, indistinguishable medley of chants came in snatches from different directions of the parade ground. The atmosphere was electric. It threw the occupants of the minibus into a panic.

"What do we do if we get split up?"

"Can you keep my purse for me, honey?"

"Where are the rest rooms?"

"Just stick together, stick together – and make for the grandstand," barked Barney. "Honey," he said to me, kindly, "you might like to stay with us. It looks a bit wild out there."

I saw the group make a beeline for the grandstand, which was sanctuary to row upon row of white faces. The area in front of it was empty. The crowds and the processions had swarmed off to other parts of the arena, but the spectators sat religiously in their wooden seats waiting for the spectacle to come to them. Eventually, the show manager felt duty-bound to make an announcement.

"Dear guests in the grandstand," he said after careful deliberation. "You are kindly invited to join the people on the parade ground. We don't think you'll be able to see anything from up there."

Slowly, the tourists came down. Their reluctance was understandable, if misplaced. The atmosphere on the ground was volatile and intimidating, and the various tribal groups that ranged throughout the crowd were flaunting illegal axes and spears. The warriors' faces were painted in horrifying blacks and death-defying yellows and reds, with bloodshot eyes and lips stained red with betelnut. But this display was aimed primarily at the competition, not the tourists. They were warriors dancing for the spirits of their ancestors, the glory of their clan and the honour of the past and the present.

The tourists, though, were still mistrustful and sometimes their nervousness proved irresistible to the warriors. An American, crouching on the ground in front of the bandstand, was taking a picture of an Asaro Mudman in a bulbous head-mask who had obligingly raised his spear in a warlike pose, when all of a sudden, the Mudman lunged at the photographer as if to run him through. The American scuttled for cover and the Mudman had to remove his mask because he was laughing so much.

Before long, Akunai had been swept up by the inevitable

flurry of *wantoks* who had tracked him down in the crowd. There were only a few groups actually competing from the Eastern Highlands – most clans were saving their energy and money for next year's show, which would be held in Goroka – but there were plenty of Eastern Highlanders who had come to watch and take notes in order to out-do the Western Highlands spectacle next year. With an apologetic wave, Akunai was sucked up into the throng and I was left to wander at leisure with my camera from one cultural group to the next.

There were men from the Wahgi Valley in head-dresses of black plumes several feet long that shook and trembled; they danced and wheeled about like courting birds. They had taken feathers from all the different kinds of birds of paradise – Princess Stephanie, King of Saxony, Sicklebill, Superbs and Magnificents – and combined them with red and green parrot feathers and bands of green scarab beetles. There were columns of men from Mendi, like the tribe we had tangled with on the Porgera road, marching with military precision, as ferocious as their compatriots had seemed several weeks before. Their feet shook the ground like a passing earthquake. There was the 'Dead Body Carrying Party' from Simbu – some of them painted with yellow clay like the flaking skin of a corpse; they held switches of leaves to flick away the flies from their rotting flesh. Others of their party were covered in black paint picked out by a gleaming white skeleton, and their hands were splayed with splints of bamboo like outstretched claws. They moved on tiptoe – in slow motion – like ghosts. In another group from Simbu, some of the warriors had covered half their body in talcum powder, while the other half was jet black with charcoal and burnt-tyre grease; like human eclipses, they appeared and disappeared as they whirled about.

But the dancers were tired. This was the third day of the performance, and they looked weary as they fought their way around the parade ground for the hundredth time. At intervals, when the drum-beating and the chanting and the marching let up, *wantoks* would come forward with slices of cucumber or a cigarette, or to remove the heavy head-dresses for a moment's relief.

Elsewhere on the parade ground, there were groups wearing non-traditional costumes. One, calling themselves the Beex Police or Minj Dustboys, had painted their bodies in a bizarre parody of the old *kiap* uniform. They had epaulettes on their bare shoulders and the leader had painted a sash across his chest, with a cluster of medals above his left nipple. They wore short black skirts, big belts and berets, false moustaches and painted-on boots and socks. But they carried real *home-guns* of the sort I had seen at Goroka police station.

There was freelance decoration among the spectators too: an old man with a biro though his nose; children in head-dresses of tinsel and Christmas decorations; a warrior in all his finery and a striped tie as well; a woman in a reed skirt and Playtex bra; and a man wearing women's earrings and Y-fronts. Elsewhere, a police badge or a cigarette packet took pride of place in a head-dress and traditional tribal gear was enhanced by the addition of shades or trainers.

This was not what most foreign spectators liked to see.

"I think it's terrible they've started to use all these western things," said one disgruntled tourist. "They've become so . . . so corrupt."

She was having trouble selecting subjects for her camera. "I can see Coke cans and cigarette packets in the States," she complained. "It's not why I've come to PNG."

She seemed to sum up the attitude of many of the tourists. They expected to find a primitive Garden of Eden untouched by aspects of their own world. For a couple of weeks they wanted to immerse themselves in the fantasy of another life, something that they could record and neatly categorise once they were back home. Naked warriors who drank Coke or were *au fait* with a camera were not part of the deal. But Papua New Guinea was a country on the move. There was energy and imagination in this adapting of new ideas, and a seasonable spirit of exploitation to match the challenges of the outside world.

Someone dressed in an orange bear suit was giving away paper hats from a Pepsi Cola float beneath a sign: 'Pepsi – the choice of a New Generation'. In order to drink from his bottle, a man in the queue removed the feather he had threaded through his upper lip.

"*Em i gutpela sing-sing,*" he remarked happily.

It was about three o'clock and the contestants were due to be judged. The crowd was cordoned off and several groups entered the arena to strut their stuff for the last time. All at once, there was an air of mounting tension, and scuffles broke out amongst the spectators. Tour groups were herded back to their buses and an administrator appealed for calm over the loudspeakers. No one seemed to know how or when the results would be announced: some people thought they might be delayed until the following day to avoid confrontation; others thought the judges had decided to call a draw. As time drew on, with no announcement from the judges in the stand, the crowd grew restive and boisterous.

"There'll be a riot any second now," said a befeathered warrior standing beside me.

I wondered how he could be so sure.

"I'm undercover policeman. People have been talking all day. It won't be good show if there isn't a fight. Perhaps you should get to your hotel before it starts."

I took his advice and began to make my way through the dancers towards the road. The smell of cooking oil on hot bodies was overpowering. A sense of aimlessness pervaded the crowd and began to assert itself like a *rascal* on the loose. Akunai could have been anywhere.

Suddenly, a shout went up and people began to stampede. Puffs of dust trailed above our heads in the wind and I realised it was tear gas. People were screaming and running in all directions, looking back over their shoulders as if pursued by some fearful monster. Children were snatched up into their fathers' arms or gripped fiercely by the hand and hurried off into the trees; most of them, though, were laughing with the thrill of it all. We ran through a cloud of smoke that had vaporised like a genie on the road before us. Immediately, my eyes began to prickle and my lips felt swollen and numb; there was a dry, acidic smell in my nostrils and a sharp pain in my sinuses.

"This way, this way," said someone by my right shoulder, and I veered off blindly towards a convoy of waiting cars. I was bundled into a car with some other bewildered tourists and driven off at full speed towards our hotel.

The crowds had slowed to their usual amble and people were walking about as if nothing had happened. Then suddenly they started running again – this time in another direction. Ahead of us, by a traffic junction, was a gang of truculent young men. They were dancing and chanting, and thrusting their spears at an invisible foe. When he saw them, our driver accelerated.

"Hold tight," he said, as we screeched over the crossroads. There was the metallic thud of missiles hitting the bodywork and one well-aimed stone cracked the back window.

"*Rascals,*" shouted our driver, "they can see damn well I'm an official."

Back in the hotel, the atmosphere seemed cotton-wool safe. Most of the guests had missed all the excitement and carried on writing postcards blithely. The receptionist was secretly triumphant.

"Not one person killed this year," she whispered. "That's very good for Mt Hagen's record. Very good for PNG's image in the Pacific Games. The riot will stop as soon as it rains," she added. "Round about five o'clock. Everyone will go home when they start to get wet."

Another Highland day was taking a curtain call when Akunai returned; he had had adventures of his own and only just made it back by hitching a lift in a dumper truck from Porgera. The sky was purple with storm clouds and the mountains were lit with familiar flickers of lightning. A fresh wind rustled the thatch over the walkways and it began to rain. It was exactly five o'clock.

That night, to celebrate the end of three days and a consistently full house, the hotel manager laid on a performance by the group which had won the Best Band Award at the Highland Show. His guests assembled in party mood. "Bravo," shouted my old friend Barney Rubble, rising from his feet as the Mt Ogar Point Brothers took their places.

The band wore lap-laps, flip-flops and brightly coloured

bilum hats with a few feathers stuck in them for good measure. They beamed with pleasure at their welcome. The musicians included two guitarists and a *kundu* drummer, but the main instruments were two sets of white plastic sewage pipes cut to different lengths and strapped together into combinations three pipes deep and three high; the longest stretched ten feet across the floor, like part of a monster Andean flute. Two of the musicians sat astride the pipes, took off their flip-flops and, at a nod, struck up a great, thunderous beat, slapping the rubber soles with furious energy against the open ends of the pipes.

The room was transformed by their music. People tapped their feet and clapped, and soon the first dancers hit the floor, gyrating in an uneasy European style to the strumming Papuan guitars.

"Thank you," said the band leader breathlessly at the end of the first song. "I'm afraid we have to wait a few seconds between songs so our shoes can cool down." The drainpipe drummers were waving their flip-flops about and tapping them experimentally. There was a faint smell of burning rubber.

"But I'll take this time to introduce a new song, very popular at the moment, called 'Happy to be in PNG', and we'd like to dedicate it to all of you for coming here from overseas. We hope you have wonderful time in our country."

The tour guide sitting next to me leapt up and dragged me onto the dance floor. People were now pushing back the sofas for more room, and guests from town seemed to have arrived for the party. I found myself dancing with a Huli warrior who was jogging around like a whirling dervish. He wore a ceremonial wig and a net skirt and leaves, and carried a cassowary club chained to his waist; a *bilum* was slung across his chest and there were bands of leaves around his calves and upper arms. I

237

gestured to Akunai to join us, but he shook his head adamantly and laughed.

"It's good party here," shouted the Wigman. "*Planti bia!*"

"Why are there no Huli groups here?" I shouted back. "I didn't see any of them at the show."

"My people having clan war back in Tari," he said. "They stay behind to fight. But I am here to represent them. This my brother's wig." And he whirled off towards our table, his wig slightly askew like an inebriated judge. Before I knew it, he had helped himself to a glass of wine and thrust another in my hand.

"We drink to tribal war," he shouted, "and my brothers in the fight, so their arrows shoot straight."

"To tribal war," I echoed, and he clinked my glass so violently it cracked the rim.

That evening in Mt Hagen, everything seemed to merge into harmonious confusion – *waitman* and *blakskin*, dancing and fighting, tribesman and tourist. Music and drinking and laughter overpowered my doubts for the future of PNG, along with my misgivings about its past.

Suddenly, I realised our journey was over. Akunai and I saluted each other and our achievements, he with his first SP for two years, me well into my second bottle of Chardonnay.

"See you in England," Akunai said. "Give me a few years, I'll be coming over to run your country."

"Or perhaps we can meet up in New York," I replied, "when you're a fat cat at the UN."

"Yeah," he laughed. "Who knows?

EPILOGUE

Kam Bek Long Kutubu Lodge

Of all the places Akunai and I had visited, Lake Kutubu preyed on me most. Over the next couple of years, as the Soviet Union crumbled and the euphoria of German unification gave way to sober realism, I wondered how Lake Kutubu was coping with its own cultural revolution. The road would be complete and the oil terminal at Moro in full operation. Perhaps it was bringing Kisa the regular custom he deserved, the 'boom business' and 'fringe benefits' the villagers had hoped for. Were there settlements now, and *rascals*? Or just the gradual change in pace from dugout to motorised canoe?

Akunai had heard nothing of Kutubu's fate. But he had written twice with news of his own. He had not been successful in applying for a post at the UN, and a change of administration at provincial government level had also lost him his job as adviser. He had found, instead, a position to which he was far better suited – editor on a new national newspaper in Port Moresby. This meant commuting weekly from his beloved Highlands down to the capital, but the challenge and satisfaction he got from his work amply rewarded him for the time he lost with his family.

Then, in December 1993, I was given the opportunity to visit the Highlands for a week. My first thought was to ask Akunai to come too, but sadly he could not risk taking time off to *go wokabaut*. I would see him on my way through Moresby, but I would have to make my last pilgrimage to the Highlands alone.

As we had flown in to Kutubu on our last trip, I planned to walk there this time, from the north. It would give me a chance to acclimatise, to recognise any changes in the area, and also to pass through the Tari Valley – home of the Huli Wigman I had danced with in Mt Hagen.

The notorious Tari weather took its time to clear as I waited impatiently in the lounge of one of the commercial air-freight companies in Mt Hagen. Some things were already different. The domestic airline, Talair, which had featured so dependably on my last trip had vanished. The ex-pat owner had crossed swords with the government and, in a fit of pique, had flown all his planes to Australia and sold them. The Talair offices in the Highlands were vacant, with blank vouchers littering the desks. Islands Airways and Islands Aviation – Talair's old competitors from the coast – were finding it hard to accommodate the complicated traffic demands of the Highlands. Their timetables changed from one day to the next and were available only as photocopies from the odd stationery shop. Passengers checked in for their flights at the back of a ute in the airstrip parking lot.

One of my fellow passengers was an engineering consultant on his way back to the Porgera gold mine. The gold deposits had outstripped even the early optimistic forecasts, he told me. A staggering 1.5 million ounces had been recovered during 1992, which, at three hundred and eighty pounds per ounce, resulted in revenues for the company of about five hundred and seventy million pounds. Around 1.2 million ounces were expected this year. The underground-drilling operation was expected to be over in another three years, but the open-cast mine at the top of the mountain, where Busybee, Akunai and I had found ourselves one chilly afternoon, would be working until the turn of the century.

However, the project was still prone to what the consultant called tribal interference. The provincial-government buildings in Wabag had been burned down earlier in the year and, some months previously, a riot at one of the Porgera camps had disrupted work for several days. The biggest problem had been an outbreak of tribal war at Laiagam, another town on the new road south of Wabag, which had left large numbers of the local Porgera workforce dead, in hospital or in jail.

Papua New Guinea: *plus ça change*, I thought with some comfort as the Bandeirante scraped several hours late into the Tari Basin. As we turned for the final approach, it became clear that it was not only the Engans who were still flexing their bows: the patches of smoke we had seen from two thousand feet were not the innocent emissions of village cooking or *kunai* burning, but the product of war.

The Tari Valley is one of the most magical in the Highlands. Fifteen miles from end to end and about seven miles at its widest, it is intensively cultivated with gardens of *kaukau* mounds, and there are natural copses and shade trees in profusion. The Highland passion for floriculture is evident in banks of hibiscus and sunflowers, datura and bougainvillea. The Dagla River gushes cold and clear across the valley floor from sources in the mountains to the east, its tributaries providing villages with deep, secluded bathing pools and good fishing.

But the basin is also characterised by its occupants' readiness to do battle. The villages here are mini-fortresses, surrounded by serious defence walls, the land criss-crossed by ditches as deep and as sheer as the trenches at Ypres. Tari had seen an acceleration of tribal fighting in recent years, and the cause was almost always some boundary dispute. In the past, the Huli, like other Highlanders, had fought over accidents, bride prices, theft or injury, but an increasing population in the valley had begun to put more and more pressure on clan land. The current war, for instance, had its origins in an ancient clan-land dispute that had re-erupted with unusual violence and consumed the whole valley. The quarrel had spread like wildfire, inflaming clans on the periphery of the argument and dividing loyalties. Neighbours and *wantoks* had been walking into Tari for days to join up. No one knew how it would end, but the days were surely numbered when the Highlanders would be able, or allowed, to fight it out. The time would come when even the Huli would have to submit to western-style compromises.

However, for the present, the Huli were shifting between old and new with ease. There were old men wearing bark-cloth aprons along with officers' caps handed down from the Second World War. Young bloods with moss in their hair, and eagles' wings sprouting from their temples like Asterix the Gaul, sported ET T-shirts. Some of the men even wore the famous Huli wigs made from human hair and shaped like up-turned boats.

The valley did not seem a place to linger, so I took a PMV up to Ambua Lodge, one of PNG's most renowned tourist hotels, in the hope that I might find a guide there who could take me to Kutubu. On the way, we passed some warriors resting by the roadside after the first battle of the day. They were sucking cucumbers, like rugby players with oranges at half-time.

Enviably situated at the top of the six-thousand-foot pass, Ambua Lodge enjoyed breathtaking views of the valley. As I'd hoped, the hotel manager was able to recommend a guide for my trek; when Thompson Tamule turned up to meet me, however, he was not impressed by the route I proposed to take to Lake Kutubu. He was a handsome man, tall even for a Huli, with a trim moustache. He studied my battered topographic map and shook his head, looking grave and disappointed. "*Em i longwe tumas,*" he said.

The manager was surprised. It was a week's easy walk out of the valley down to the lake and Thompson knew the way well. A brief conference revealed Thompson's real concern: the route crossed a large section of territory belonging to clans who had just entered the Tari war on the side of Thompson's enemies. It would be impossible to find anyone from Ambua – including Thompson himself, he said – who would be willing to take that route.

The only alternative was to take a PMV on to the town of Nipa and make a shorter, but much more challenging, trek across the limestone karst that formed the eastern barrier to the lake. This was the infamous 'Broken Bottle Country' that Akunai and I had originally seen from the comfort of a helicopter on our way to Kutubu from Porgera gold mine, and that the Australian Jack Hides had first encountered in 1935 on his Kikori River patrol. It had been the last blank space remaining on the map of the island and most people with an inkling of the area could see why. Sir Hubert Murray, governor at the time, described Hides's expedition as 'the most difficult and dangerous patrol ever carried out in the whole island of New Guinea'. In those days, the terrain was only part of the challenge; Hides had been attacked five times in five months, and 'harassed' on innumerable occasions in this particular area.

However, Thompson's stalling had nothing to do with either geography or history. He wanted to stay in Tari so he could fight alongside his *wantoks*. He was swayed at last by the promise of a return plane flight from the oil terminal at Moro that would get him back home to join the fray after an absence of only four days. We shook hands on the deal and agreed to meet on the road outside the lodge gates at seven the next morning.

By eight-thirty, there was still no sign of Thompson on the road. I sat there, irritation and nerves undermining my resolve, when a figure in a bright orange boiler suit and black wellington boots, carrying a frog-green umbrella, finally came lolloping through the *kunai*. Thompson did not apologise and was clearly chuffed by the figure he cut in his professional going-away clothes. A smaller man in shorts and a shabby T-shirt was with him.

"This is my *brata,* Komite, coming with us to carry your *ruksak,*" he said.

It was only when I was sitting next to him in the PMV that I noticed there were traces of face-paint in Thompson's moustache. "We been fighting our enemies," he said. "Yesterday they burn down my house. So early this morning I put on my feathers and my paint-things and pull out my *home-gun* and go and shoot them." Komite could speak no English but he smiled triumphantly.

"You know, you've chosen best guide in this area," continued Thompson. "I'm *big man* in these whereabouts. Maybe you give me your *ruksak* and other things when you go *pinis* – when you leave *hia.*"

The Thompson in command of a single white woman was very different from the reticent, obliging figure he'd cut with the hotel manager at Ambua Lodge. I began to steel myself against overfamiliarity and tried to forge a respectful distance between us.

We spent our first night on the outskirts of a village near Nipa. The village was gearing itself up for the consecration of a new Catholic church, and the place resounded with people and the screaming of one hundred and fifty pigs being slaughtered. With some difficulty, we managed to persuade two villagers to forego the great *mumu* at hand and show us the new route to Lake Kutubu. Torrential rain had washed away the main bridge on our trail and Thompson seemed extremely vague about how to get round this difficulty.

The next morning, we plunged into thick montane forest almost as soon as we left the village. Thompson was too grand to shoulder any baggage himself and carried only his umbrella and *bilum*, which was several times lighter than my own. He put his orange boiler suit and wellies into my rucksack on his brother's back so they wouldn't get muddy, and idly brought up the rear. The guides from the village shot an unnerving distance ahead of us with boxes of provisions on their backs.

The path was a near-vertical version of the bush trails I had crashed along by the shores of Lake Kutubu. Dense, dripping foliage crawling with ants was draped across it. The mulch on the forest floor wriggled with leeches, waving and stretching for warm blood as they sensed the vibrations of oncoming mammals. After three hours, I was too tired to pay attention to the black lozenges feeding on my legs; it was easier to keep walking and let them drop off when they had finished, and to derive a little morbid satisfaction from watching the raspberry-ripple effect creep down my socks. By the same token, it became easier to track the local guides ahead of us: at every junction in the path, on every fallen log, or wherever they had taken a rest, was a bloody mash of leeches to signal where the guides had finally lost their patience and scraped their legs clean with their *busnaips*.

As we continued through the forest, my companions daubed their faces with clay and put curling fingers of fern in their hair, addressing the jungle as Simi and Sandap had done three years before. Once, we came to a sacred clearing and the local guides stopped to murmur an incantation to the spirits. Thompson crossed himself for good measure.

That evening, we camped under the roof of an old hunting shelter by a magical, mild-tempered river. There were great mossy boulders in the water, covered with white flowers like a fairy tale, and banks of fireflies that lit up the surrounding forest as night fell. We had trekked for nine relentless hours and forded three rivers. The local guides retrieved secret hordes of dry wood and made a fire and a miniature *mumu* to cook *kaukau*, while Thompson opened some packets of noodles to make soup.

Only Komite was untouched by the exhilaration of hot food and a bed for the night. He stared glassy-eyed at the fire and hugged his chest. I asked Thompson if anything was wrong. "He's feeling pain," came the nonchalant reply. "He was shot by an arrow on morning we left in PMV to Nipa. Komite was pulling out the arrow himself but little bit still stay inside him, make him pain."

But why, I asked, had he not gone to hospital in Tari?

"Hospital charging sixty kina now to remove arrows," said Thompson. "So trying to stop tribal wars in Tari. But people just remove arrows theirselves. And hospital is a dangerous place.

You can be lying there and all your *wantoks* sitting around the bed and your enemy says 'Hi! Now I know where you are!' and he comes in and kills you all. Much better to stay at home. Take your medicine in your own house."

I remembered with sickening regret that I had fastened my rucksack so tightly on Komite that he had gasped. I made Thompson promise that he would send his brother to the clinic at Lake Kutubu, where there would be no enemies to ambush him. Meanwhile, while the rest of us collapsed in exhausted sleep, Komite sat up, uncomplaining, all night.

The following day brought more of the same: endless limestone ridges, one after the other, each step sending shock waves through the muscles. I remembered how remote and spectacular the Broken Bottles had looked from the helicopter, and spared a few sympathetic thoughts for the first patrol ever to penetrate this jungle and reach the lake. I began to anticipate the simple luxuries of Kutubu Lodge like someone lost in the wilderness for weeks: a hot shower, a cold beer, some good food, a comfortable chair, dry clothes. Even if Akunai had been able to spare the time, this was no trip for him. But I missed his company, and regretted that when Kisa and I sat down together over a steaming pile of yabbies, Akunai would not be there to voice his disgust.

Walking for hour upon hour, I reflected on my previous trip and PNG three years on. Little seemed to have changed in the Eastern Highlands considering the developments we had witnessed. Goroka was much the same. Old women grumbled that young girls were now slinging their *bilums* over their shoulders so as not to mess up their hair. Clans which had sold their land for the building of Goroka in the 1950s were trying to extract further payments from the government by threatening to sabotage the town's water and electricity supplies. This year's

Highlands Show, back in Mt Hagen, had been cancelled because of *rascal* activity in the area, and everyone in Goroka was doubling their efforts to put on an even bigger show to mark their superiority. Goroka still had its *rascal* problems, and police had burned down several villages in the Kainantu region suspected of harbouring criminals.

But these were indications of normality, not of change. Had the people of Goroka shown signs of constancy, of predictability, of acceptance, then that would have signalled a change of heart. As it was, the spirit of rivalry and defiance was still keen in the east – albeit modified by the activities of modern life – and if Tari was anything to go by, so it was in the west, too. My fears about the survival of Lake Kutubu began to diminish.

As we stumbled on over the Broken Bottles, the temperature of the forest changed almost imperceptibly. There were sago and black palm and tigaso trees now – native species of lowland forest – and butterflies and insects. We passed through a clearing, all that was left of a village whose occupants had been wiped out by malaria.

Several hours later we were surprised by a sow that crashed across our path with three piglets in tow – our first sign of civilisation. Soon there were gardens and fallow clearings, traces of campfires and even handrails and stepping stones to help young and old over the terrain. We passed our first villagers, and at last, nine hours after we had set out, we scaled our final ridge to the busy village of Yalanda and caught our first sight of Lake Kutubu.

Despite all my memories, I wasn't prepared for the beauty of that first glimpse. The water gleamed a deep royal blue in a coronet of mountains, the familiar shape of Wasemi Island lying in the middle like an emerald on satin. Beyond it, way into the distance, towered the hazy volcanic cone of Mt Bosavi. I almost ran to keep up with the guides now. I was worried that Kisa might not be expecting us at the lodge; that the booking, sent via radio from Ambua after we had left, might have been cancelled; that Chevron staff or Porgera employees would have taken our beds.

There was a new tractor road leading down from Yalanda, and after five miles it connected us to the gigantic new highway from Mendi. It was difficult to imagine that this, too, had been impenetrable forest only last year; that I had walked part of it with Simi and Sandap when there were only little red markers predicting this great white *haiwe*. Only the stumps of mighty trees – six feet in diameter and two days' hard felling for one man – hinted at the scale of the violation. My feeling of unease intensified and, sure enough, a few miles further down the road we were approached by a couple of villagers who warned us of *rascals*.

A group of them had been seen, armed with *home-guns* and *busnaips*, wandering down the road in our direction. The Nipa guides looked anxious and began to talk of turning back; Thompson was in a quandary. For me, the choice was quite plain: I could no more climb back up over those mountains than I could conquer Everest. Kisa was only two miles away downhill, and wild horses, let alone a band of *rascals*, would not stand between me and Kutubu Lodge. Thompson and Komite, and eventually the guides, seemed persuaded by my show of resolve and we cantered on down towards the lake, keeping a sharp eye out for an ambush.

We never caught up with the *rascals*. But my relief was tempered by the sight that greeted us when we turned off onto the little path leading down to Tage Point. The beautiful plantations that had once graced the slopes behind the lodge were reverting to jungle. We had to slash our way through the old pineapple gardens and vegetable plots, past crumbling sheds and water tanks eaten by rust. In the crepuscular light, Kutubu Lodge loomed on the promontory like a great dark hull – black, empty and uninviting. The *kukhaus* round the back was locked, the guest rooms and the volleyball court were as silent as the grave.

Trying to contain my despair, I hurried up the steps to the veranda and fell through the rotten floorboards. The handrail came off in my hand. Inside, treading carefully on only the joists, the five of us looked vainly for any sign of life. In Kisa's office I found a notice scrawled on the blackboard nine months before: '15-3-93 – five Japanise tourist, two nights'. There was also a polite reminder: 'Kisa – remember to submit your monthly accounts at the end of the month'.

The visitors' book with its appreciative messages was nowhere to be seen. Behind the bar, the fridge was padlocked with a heavy chain; hoping at least for a warm Fanta or, better still, an SP, I searched frantically for the key. When the chain was finally released, the door fell with a clunk onto the floor and there was nothing inside but mould.

Thompson was sitting slumped in an empty rattan chair, observing my futile efforts and picking his fingernails. Komite sat outside on the steps, his face ashen beneath traces of yellow clay. I tried to pay off the Nipa guides but they argued about the price; at last, they left with double the wages we had agreed on and beaming, unrepentant smiles.

Thompson yawned and stretched his legs. "Maybe there's someone in nearby village can come and make supper. I very tired."

Suddenly, under the strain of bitter disappointment, my temper snapped. I herded Thompson out of the lodge, barely holding back my tears, and shouted at him to go and look for someone. He lolloped off reluctantly, asserting his authority once again in his European wellies and orange boiler suit. Komite and I sat in silence on the steps, where once Akunai and Kisa and I had sat, and watched the mountains across the lake draw in the last rays of sunlight.

In my worst premonitions I had imagined Lake Kutubu crowded with people or humming with motors. I could never have guessed that the road would bring nothing. Years down the line, perhaps, my forebodings would be vindicated: there would be settlements and supermarkets, Toyota trucks and the smell of fast food. But nothing could be as awful as this present ambivalent void.

Thompson eventually managed to flush out a Foi villager, who brought us *kakaruk* crackers, more noodle soup, the last cans of Coke from the Wasemi *tredstoa* and snippets of news about Kisa and the lodge. The last visitors had come nearly a year ago; the Japanese referred to on the blackboard had never showed up; Kisa had left for Mendi several months back and no one knew when or if he would return. He had fallen out with the management at Chevron and they had withdrawn their support for the lodge. Other guests were frightened off by the advent of *rascals*, who had been drifting into the region. Only the previous night they had held up a school and a new mission station on the headland near Tage Point. It would probably be only one or two days before the *rascals* arrived at Kutubu Lodge and tore it to pieces.

As for the Wasemi *longhaus*, that bastion of Foi tradition, the villagers themselves had burned it down, turning in on themselves, it seemed, like scorpions under a glass. Where the Huli Wigmen had been numerous and vigorous enough to resist some of the forces of change, the less assertive Foi had been driven to cultural suicide.

Every clan, every valley, every region in the Highlands had its own pace of change; its own objections; its own solutions. If there was one thing I was at last beginning to realise, it was that there was no pattern to it all. I was fifty years too late to see the initial reactions of the Eastern Highlanders to industry and commerce, to shifting populations and the opening up of traditional worlds. That was already *long taim bifo.* Kainantu and Goroka, even as far as Mt Hagen in the Western Highlands, were spinning along now in the slipstream of the late twentieth century; they had already reached their compromises. Only in geographical backwaters like Wabag and Lake Kutubu, out of reach of the big valleys, was it possible to catch the wobbly adjustments of a culture still changing course; to witness the awkward manoeuvring of people bumping up against the western world's Pandora's box.

I spent my last night at Lake Kutubu on a musty mattress in one of the old guest rooms, sleeping in my shoes and all my clothes for fear of *rascals.* In the early hours of the morning there came a sudden ripping, crashing sound from outside. I thought I was under attack and scurried to prepare myself for flight. But within moments I realised what had happened: one of the huge old buttressed trees had groaned its last and toppled headlong, inches from my balcony. It seemed the forest itself was giving up the ghost.

GLOSSARY

arapela – another

bagarap – (lit. buggered-up) broken

balus – bird, airplane

banaras – (lit. bow and arrows) bow

bia – beer

big man – a natural-born leader, recognised as such because of some innate ability, physical prowess, education or other advantage. There is no hereditary leadership entitlement within a clan; rather, a big man rises to the fore through general consent. Often the mark of a *big man* is his ability to give away wealth, especially at ritual celebrations or as *payback*.

bikpela – big

bilas – from the English 'flash': finery, ornaments, decoration (hence *bilas bilong sing-sing* means ornaments worn at a festival); and as verb – to show off, or be conceited.

bilong – belong, belonging to

bilum – traditional string bag made originally from bark or seisal but more recently from colourful nylon thread. Can also mean 'womb' (babies are carried in both!).

binatang – insect, edible grub

bokis ais – (lit. icebox) refrigerator

brata – brother

bus – bush, countryside

bus kanaka – from the Fijian *kanaka*, meaning 'native'; hence 'bush

native', a derogatory term suggesting a savage or uncivilised person (often used by Eastern Highlanders to describe Western Highlanders).
busnaip – bushknife, machete

dimanples – (lit. die-man-place) limbo
disil pawa – diesel power

em nau – (lit. him now) appreciative remark

foa wil draiv – four-wheel drive

gavman – government
gol main – gold mine

Hailans – Highlands
Hailans Kalsarel So – Highlands Cultural Show
haiwe – highway
hankisip – handkerchief
haus draiva – (lit. house-driver) truck-driver's cab
haus spaida – (lit. house-spider) web
home-gun – homemade shot gun

kago – (lit. cargo) supplies, luggage, etc. A common belief, particularly in coastal areas, is that the ancestors (*ol tumbuna*) are responsible for sending gifts to their descendants from wherever it is they have gone to after death. When the Red Cross dropped supplies in the South Pacific during the Second World War, many villagers believed the chocolate, cigarettes and food rations were gifts from the dead – particularly since Christian missionaries had begun teaching the principle of heavenly reward, and these gifts were coming from the sky, labelled with the sign of the cross! Several bizarre cargo cults developed as a result. Generally, however, a kind of cargo-cult attitude prevails throughout tribal New Guinea. It is an optimistic, Micawber-like belief that 'something will turn up' and that 'there's more where that came from'.
kakaruk – chicken

kam bek – (lit. come back) return

kamap – to come up, appear, rise, reach

kantri – country

kauboi – cowboy

kaukau – sweet potato

kiap – from the English 'captain'; a government official or district officer in colonial times (hence *haus kiap* was the government official's house).

kina – valuable mother-of-pearl shell used for bartering; hence present-day Papua New Guinean paper currency.

kisim poto – take a photo

kukboi – cookboy

kukhaus – cookhouse

kunai – sword grass (*Imperata arundinacea*); grass in general, meadow, grassland.

kundu – drum

lap-lap – wrap-around garment, loincloth, sarong

long – (used for almost any preposition) in, on, at, to, from, with, by, etc

longhaus – segregated communal dwelling house

long taim bifo – (lit. long time before) in the distant past, usually referring to prehistory or the time before first contact and colonisation.

misis – any European woman, married or not

mumu – an earth oven, or cooking pit; the traditional Highland method of cooking. Nowadays, it is most often used for cooking a large quantity of food, especially pigs, on ceremonial occasions.

muruk – cassowary bird

nambawan – (lit. number one) the best, excellent

nogut – (lit. no good) bad, wicked, evil; hence *taim nogut* means bad weather.

pati – party

payback – compensation paid by one clan to another, usually in the form of pigs and paper money, to atone for some wrong-doing. This could be theft, rape, murder or simply an accident.

pikinini – child

piksa – picture, photo

pinis – finish, end; hence *go pinis* means leave for good.

planti – plenty

plismastas – police officers

PMV – Public Motor Vehicle

raifel – rifle

rascal – euphemism for a criminal or law-breaker, ranging from petty thief to rapist and axe-murderer

rot – road

ruksak – rucksack

saksak – sago

sanguma – from the Melanesian *sang-guma*; originally described a method of poisoning by sorcerers in which the victim was mesmerised and then poisoned by thorns. More loosely describes any form of black magic performed to terrify, mesmerise or inflict pain upon a victim.

sekonhan klos – second-hand clothes (mostly donated from Australia and sold cheaply in tradestores)

singaut – (lit. sing out) a call, a cry, to call – a kind of yodel used to communicate between villages, across gorges etc.

sing-sing – festival. Implies dancing, singing and, often, feasting.

skulmankis – school children

sori – sorry

spe – spare

spias – spears or arrows

stesin – station

strongpela – strong

taia – tyre

taim – time, weather

taim bilong masta – (lit. time of the white man, or European) any time from the 1840s on the coast, or as late as the 1960s in the Highlands (whenever the first government patrol posts were established), up to independence in 1975.

tanget – shrub (*Taetsia fructicosa*) with distinctive red and green leaves, used in sorcery and for sending messages. Tucked into the belt, they are used by Highland men to cover their buttocks (ex-pats refer to tanget as 'ass grass').

tok pisin – (lit. talk pidgin) the lingua franca of PNG – a simplified language taken mainly from English, but with a smattering of German and some local and South Pacific vocabulary.

tok ples – (lit. talk place) local dialect or language, of which there are around 750 distinct examples (two-fifths of the world's total languages) in PNG. A clan is often identified as those who can speak the same language (see *wantok*).

tredstoa – tradestore

tripela – three

tru – true, real; truly, really; very

tumas – (lit. too much) very, very much

tumbuna – term from the island of New Britain meaning ancestors, grandparents etc. *Ples bilong ol tumbuna* means ancestral burial grounds.

tupela – two

wantok – (lit. one talk) anyone who can speak the same native language, or *tok ples*; hence (commonly) a relative or friend. The further a person is from home, the more loosely the definition is applied. Outside one's native region, a *wantok* may be someone from a neighbouring clan; in the capital, a *wantok* may be someone from the same province; and abroad, anyone from the same country.

wasman – guard

wokabaut – (lit. walkabout) journey, hike

LONELY PLANET JOURNEYS

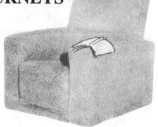

JOURNEYS is a unique collection of travellers' tales – published by the company that understands travel better than anyone else.

It is a series for anyone who has ever experienced – or dreamed of – the magical moment when they encountered a strange culture or saw a place for the first time. They are tales to read while you're planning a trip, while you're on the road or while you're in an armchair, in front of a fire.

Lonely Planet guidebooks have always gone beyond providing simple nuts-and-bolts information, so it is a short step to JOURNEYS, a new series of outstanding titles that will explore our planet through the eyes of a fascinating and diverse group of international travellers.

JOURNEYS books will catch the spirit of a place, illuminate a culture, recount a crazy adventure, or introduce a fascinating way of life. They will always entertain, and always enrich the experience of travel.

SEAN & DAVID'S LONG DRIVE
Sean Condon

Sean and David are young townies who
have rarely strayed beyond city limits.
One day, for no good reason, they set out
to discover their homeland, and what
follows is a wildly entertaining adventure that covers half of Australia.
Highlights include the weekly Hair Wax
Report and a Croc-Spotting with Stew
adventure.

Sean Condon has written a hilarious,
offbeat road book that mixes sharp
insights with deadpan humour and outright lies.

Sean Condon lives in Melbourne. He played drums in several
mediocre bands until he found his way into advertising and an
above-average band called Boilersuit. *Sean & David's Long Drive*
is his first book.

THE GATES OF DAMASCUS

Lieve Joris
Translated by Sam Garrett

This best-selling book is a beautifully drawn portrait of day-to-day life in modern Syria. Through her intimate contact with local people, Lieve Joris draws us into the fascinating world that lies behind the gates of Damascus. Hala's husband is a political prisoner, jailed for his opposition to the Assad regime; through the author's friendship with Hala we see how Syrian politics impacts on the lives of ordinary people.

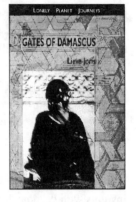

Written after the Gulf War, *The Gates of Damascus* offers a unique insight into the complexities of the Arab world.

Lieve Joris, who was born in Belgium, is one of Europe's foremost travel writers. In addition to an award-winnng book on Hungary, she has published widely acclaimed accounts of her journeys to the Middle East and Africa. *The Gates of Damascus* is her fifth book.

LOST JAPAN

Alex Kerr

Lost Japan draws on the author's personal experiences of Japan over thirty years. Alex Kerr takes his readers on a backstage tour, exploring different facets of his involvement with the country: friendships with Kabuki actors, buying and selling art, studying calligraphy, exploring rarely visited temples and shrines...

The Japanese edition of this book was awarded the 1994 Shincho Gakugei Literature Prize for the best work of non-fiction: the first time a foreigner has won this prestigious award.

Alex Kerr is an American who lives in Japan. He majored in Japanese studies at Yale, collects Japanese art and has founded his own art-dealing business. He has worked as a business consultant and also with the Oomoto Foundation, a Shinto religious group devoted to the practice and teaching of traditional Japanese arts. Simultaneously 'a foreigner' and 'an insider', Alex Kerr brings a unique perspective to writing about contemporary Japan.

RELATED TITLES
FROM LONELY PLANET

Papua New Guinea – a travel survival kit

With its coastal cities, villages perched beside mighty rivers, palm-fringed beaches and rushing mountain streams, Papua New Guinea promises memorable travel.

Bushwalking in Papua New Guinea

The best way to get to know Papua New Guinea is from the ground up – and bushwalking is the best way to travel around the rugged and varied landscape of this island.

Papua New Guinea (Pidgin) phrasebook

This is the indispensable phrasebook for travellers in Papua New Guinea and Irian Jaya.

Packed with words and phrases and an extensive vocabulary, this handy phrasebook will get you through every situation.

Indonesia – a travel survival kit

Some of the most remarkable sights and sounds in South-East Asia can be found amongst the 13,000 islands of Indonesia – this book covers the entire archipelago in detail.

Indonesian phrasebook

This pocket phrasebook is your key to finding the real Indonesia. With useful words and phrases for getting around and getting to know people, you need never be lost, or lost for words.

Indonesian audio pack

Join two travellers in Indonesia as they meet people, find accommodation, sights, eat out and sample the nightlife.

Travellers will learn essential words and phrases – and their correct pronunciation – by participating in a realistic story.

The audio pack is presented in an attractive cloth wallet made from indigenous textiles by local communities.

PLANET TALK

Lonely Planet's FREE quarterly newsletter

Every issue of PLANET TALK is packed with
up-to-date travel news and advice including:

- a letter from Lonely Planet founders Tony
  and Maureen Wheeler
- travel diary from a Lonely Planet author
  – find out what it's really like out on the road
- feature article on an important and topical
  travel issue
- a selection of recent letters from our readers
- the latest travel news from all over the world
- details on Lonely Planet's new and
  forthcoming releases

To join our mailing list contact any Lonely Planet office.

LONELY PLANET PUBLICATIONS

Australia: PO Box 617, Hawthorn 3122, Victoria
tel: (03) 9819 1877 fax: (03) 9819 6459
e-mail: talk2us@lonelyplanet.com.au

USA: Embarcadero West, 155 Filbert St, Suite 251,
Oakland, CA 94607
tel: (510) 893 8555 TOLL FREE: 800 275-8555
fax: (510) 893 8563 e-mail: info@lonelyplanet.com

UK: 10 Barley Mow Passage, Chiswick, London W4 4PH
tel: (0181) 742 3161 fax: (0181) 742 2772
e-mail: 100413.3551@compuserve.com

France: 71 bis rue du Cardinal Lemoine – 75005 Paris
tel: 1 44 32 06 20 fax: 1 46 34 72 55
e-mail: 100560.415@compuserve.com

World Wide Web: Lonely Planet is now accesible via the World
Wide Web. For travel information and an up-to-date catalogue, you
can find us at http://www.lonelyplanet.com/

THE LONELY PLANET STORY

Lonely Planet published its first book in 1973 in response to the numerous 'How did you do it?' questions Maureen and Tony Wheeler were asked after driving, bussing, hitching, sailing and railing their way from England to Australia.

Written at a kitchen table and hand collated, trimmed and stapled, *Across Asia on the Cheap* became an instant local bestseller, inspiring thoughts of another book.

Eighteen months in South-East Asia resulted in their second guide, *South-East Asia on a shoestring*, which they put together in a backstreet Chinese hotel in Singapore in 1975. The 'yellow bible' as it quickly became known to backpackers around the world, soon became *the* guide to the region. It has sold well over half a million copies and is now in its 8th edition, still retaining its familiar yellow cover.

Today there are over 180 titles, including travel guides, walking guides, language kits & phrasebooks, travel atlases and travel literature. The company is one of the largest travel publishers in the world. Although Lonely Planet initially specialised in guides to Asia, we now cover most regions of the world, including the Pacific, North America, South America, Africa, the Middle East and Europe.

The emphasis continues to be on travel for independent travellers. Tony and Maureen still travel for several months of each year and play an active part in the writing, updating and quality control of Lonely Planet's guides.

They have been joined by over 50 authors and 155 staff at our offices in Melbourne (Australia), Oakland (USA), London (UK) and Paris (France). Travellers themselves also make a valuable contribution to the guides through the feedback we receive in thousands of letters each year.

The people at Lonely Planet strongly believe that travellers can make a positive contribution to the countries they visit, both through their appreciation of the countries' culture, wildlife and natural features, and through the money they spend. In addition, the company makes a direct contribution to the countries and regions it covers. Since 1986 a percentage of the income from each book has been donated to ventures such as famine relief in Africa; aid projects in India; agricultural projects in Central America; Greenpeace's efforts to halt French nuclear testing in the Pacific; and Amnesty International.

Lonely Planet's basic travel philosophy is summed up in Tony Wheeler's comment, 'Don't worry about whether your trip will work out. Just go!'